THE REGENERATION THROUGH HERITAGE

HANDBOOK

How to use a redundant historic building
as a catalyst for change in your community

Edited by Fred Taggart
with Simon Thorpe and Lydia Wilson

WITHDRAWN

Published by Phillimore for

THE PRINCE'S REGENERATION TRUST
REGENERATION THROUGH HERITAGE

It sometimes occurs to me that the British have more heritage than is
good for them. In a country where there is so astonishingly much of
everything, it is easy to look on it as a kind of inexhaustible resource...
There is so much of it everywhere that it is easy to believe that you
can take away chunks of it... and that there will still be plenty left.
In fact, the country is being nibbled to death.

from *Notes from a Small Island* by Bill Bryson

2006

Published for the The Prince's Regeneration Trust by
Phillimore & Co. Ltd
Shopwyke Manor Barn, Chichester, West Sussex, England
www.phillimore.co.uk

ISBN 1 86077 391 5

Designed by The letter g, www.letterg.co.uk

Photography by
British Waterways; Architectural Heritage Fund; Bob Collier;
David Titchener; Tim Guthrie; RTH Photo Library.

Printed and bound in Great Britain by Herald Graphics, Reading

The Prince's Regeneration Trust is the working title of
The Prince's Regeneration Through Heritage Trust

Registered charity 1089932
A Company limited by guarantee (England 4342518)

VAT registration 858 319 490

THE
REGENERATION
THROUGH
HERITAGE
HANDBOOK

CLARENCE HOUSE

Ten years ago I established Regeneration Through Heritage in order to help communities find new sustainable uses for otherwise redundant heritage buildings. I am delighted so many of the projects it has supported are now making real progress. With passion and commitment, community groups, working in partnership with local authorities, business, regeneration agencies and heritage organisations, are achieving great things. This Handbook is based on their experience.

Sadly, many marvellous old buildings still lie unused, so there is much to do. These buildings can add so much to the quality of our lives and help give a community its unique identity. I hope this Handbook will provide encouragement and advice to concerned communities. More importantly, I hope it will *empower* people who care about where they live and help them turn concern about the neglect of heritage buildings into constructive action.

I am so grateful to English Heritage and the other sponsors for helping to fund Regeneration Through Heritage. This has made it possible to show that, with on-going support, local people working together can save much-loved buildings and make a real difference.

I would also like to thank the Heritage Lottery Fund and King Sturge for aiding the publication of this Handbook. It is much needed and, I am sure, will be much used.

ABOUT REGENERATION THROUGH HERITAGE

The United Kingdom has a magnificent legacy of historic buildings, many from the great Victorian building age when talent, architectural skill and money were lavished on buildings with often quite modest industrial or utilitarian purposes. There is such a large inheritance of good buildings that their value is not always recognised and now, with their original purpose gone, many are at risk of dereliction or demolition. Architectural heritage is being lost at an alarming rate and wonderful buildings are being swept away, often for look-alike industrial estates and anonymous business parks.

Communities everywhere are concerned by these losses and will support efforts and campaigns to adapt vacant or redundant historic buildings for new uses. With the government's policy focus now on the regeneration of urban areas and brownfield sites there is also a new awareness among decision-makers of the importance of an attractive built environment as a generator of economic wealth and social wellbeing.

The Parliamentary Select Committee on The Role of Historic Buildings in Urban Regeneration said in 2004:

> The historic environment has an important part to play in regeneration schemes, helping to create vibrant interesting areas, boosting local economies and restoring local confidence. When historic buildings, including churches and theatres, are no longer needed for their original purpose, they are capable of conversion for a wide range of other purposes.

However, in much of the country market conditions are such that there is little commercial prospect of redundant historic buildings being brought back into use. It is in these communities where local people are most likely to be able to resist loss of their heritage.

Regeneration Through Heritage (RTH) was established in 1996 by HRH The Prince of Wales to promote the sustainable re-use of historic buildings, primarily by assisting community groups and not-for-profit community-based partnerships to develop proposals for particular buildings at risk. We are a small team, part of The Prince's Regeneration Trust, and can help groups in any part of the United Kingdom.

The groups we advise have saved a wide variety of historic buildings, attracted grants and investment in excess of £30 million, and brought more than 500,000 square feet of redundant floor space into use for new housing, offices, workshops, restaurants, retail space and community facilities. Space for more than 1,000 jobs has been created. This was achieved by local people, many with little or no experience of heritage-led regeneration, who saw the potential to re-use an historic building for wider community benefit.

RTH also holds seminars and conferences about heritage-led regeneration, publishes advice and guidance, and maintains a website with examples of good practice and current projects.

Each building and group we advise is different and there is no universal formula to guarantee success. However, RTH has developed a successful methodology that will enable groups to tackle a project in a systematic and business-like way. We have a national support network of like-minded community groups, professionals, developers, academics and interested individuals, who are pleased to share their knowledge and experience with those about to embark on a project.

This Handbook is a 'route-map' for community groups and voluntary partnerships to help them through the early stages of a project to regenerate a redundant historic building. It begins with the identification of a suitable building and guides the group through to the funding application stage, when full-time professional help usually takes over. It is a tested formula based on the experience of the groups RTH supports.

The prospect of undertaking the task of restoring and re-using a historic building can seem daunting but, with on-going advice and support, this is something ordinary people can successfully accomplish to the benefit of their own community and the nation as a whole.

We hope this Handbook will show you the way and give you the confidence to have a go.

Fred Taggart
Director, Regeneration Through Heritage

Baily's Factory, Glastonbury, Somerset [case study]

Leather processing and manufacture has been an important industry in Glastonbury since before the Middle Ages, reaching its peak in the late 19th and early 20th centuries with Baily's Factory, latterly as part of the larger adjoining Morlands Company, supplying Clark's of Street. With the ending of all production the owners sought permission to redevelop the wider Morland's site, which by then incorporated Baily's.

While much of the site comprised undistinguished post-war sheds it also contained other Victorian buildings in brick and stone, and 20th-century modernist buildings, of architectural and historic value. All were unlisted and many would be demolished as part of the redevelopment. Concerned local people, supported by the Town Council, opposed the proposals at a planning inquiry and asked the Secretary of State to list the best buildings. The redevelopment scheme was not approved and while the modernist and Victorian brick buildings were not listed, the two stone-built Baily's Factory buildings were listed Grade II.

The site was acquired by the South West of England Regional Development Agency (SWERDA). In light of further local representations it agreed to retain as many as possible of the better unlisted buildings. While some of the modernist buildings in the centre of the site were cleared, it was agreed that the Victorian brick buildings and the 'Bauhaus' modernist building would be retained, if possible, and marketed separately.

Furthermore, SWERDA agreed that if the local RTH-established Partnership could develop sustainable proposals for the re-use of Baily's and establish a charitable Trust as a delivery mechanism, it would be willing to negotiate ownership.

The Partnership held a Planning Day at which options for future uses were agreed, including space for educational and community uses, and new small businesses. Key to the Partnership's success was its willingness to make the case to the owners, the planning authorities, and the local community about the importance of the Baily's Factory, and the wider Morland's site, to Glastonbury and to engage in a continuing dialogue. These efforts helped secure the future of unlisted but important historic buildings that might otherwise have been lost, and the support of SWERDA for a potential community-led regeneration project for listed buildings that were unlikely to attract a private developer.

1

FINDING A BUILDING

We all know historic buildings that have seen better days or been empty for many years. Often these buildings capture our interest and imagination because of their architecture, form and materials, or because they are reminiscent of former industrial or social activities that were once part of our community. Neglected historic buildings may have a faded glamour and beauty, but the reality is that once maintenance stops it is not long before weather and vandalism take hold and put them at risk of terminal decline and permanent loss.

Buildings at Risk registers

A building at risk may have deteriorated for many reasons. It could, for example, be subject to an inappropriate use that is causing structural damage, or have users who do not invest in its upkeep. A building may also have been subject to an application for demolition, a statutory Repairs or Urgent Works Notice, or an application to alter its historic fabric and integrity.

There are many more derelict historic buildings at risk than there are voluntary organisations to restore them. Examples can be found on Buildings at Risk registers prepared by national heritage agencies and local authorities.

England
The national Buildings at Risk register is managed by English Heritage, and includes Grade I and Grade II* buildings and is available on-line. Grade II buildings at risk are included in local registers, which are usually managed by local authorities.

Wales
The Buildings at Risk registers are managed by the local authorities, which receive grants for this purpose from Cadw: Welsh Historic Monuments. However, not all authorities keep

a register – check with the relevant conservation officer or planning department. **The Civic Trust for Wales** can also help.

Scotland
The Buildings at Risk register is managed by the **Scottish Civic Trust** and is available on-line.

Northern Ireland
The **Ulster Architectural Heritage Society (UAHS)**, with support from **Environment and Heritage Service**, compiles catalogues of buildings at risk. You can also write to the **Ulster Architectural Heritage Society** to request a free copy and it is available on-line.

Once a building has been found, what next?

An economically sustainable new use is critical to a project's success, even one on a relatively small scale: in order to survive, a building must be able to generate sufficient income to support its regular maintenance. This means that any new uses will need to provide reliable revenue, commercial rent or other income.

Other issues that will influence the development of the chosen building might include the following:
— Is there potential to develop a viable re-use proposal for the building? Is it too small or constrained by other limiting factors?
— Are there any serious environmental issues relating to the site, such as flooding or contamination problems, that will be too costly to resolve?
— Is there adequate access e.g. road, rail, water?
— Are services easily available e.g. water, sewerage?

Where to find help?

Local authorities
If the building you are interested in is on an 'at risk' register, the first step should be to telephone, visit, email or write to your local authority, setting out your concerns and interest in finding a solution. (There is an example of a suitable letter at the end of this chapter.)

Regional agencies

Also contact the regional office of your relevant heritage organisation: English Heritage, Cadw, Historic Scotland or Environment and Heritage Service in Northern Ireland. They can provide contacts for specialists and conservation organisations in your area, or, if appropriate, for national organisations. They may already have a file on the building, or contact with its owner(s). If the owner has no plans, the Regional Development Agency, or equivalent, should be supportive of proposals to sensitively restore the building to a viable new use where this helps boost the local economy.

Amenity societies

There are several national amenity societies that can offer invaluable advice. These include the Society for the Protection of Ancient Buildings, the Georgian Group, the Victorian Society, the Twentieth Century Society and the Ancient Monuments Society.

[see Contacts]   ### Association of Preservation Trusts (APT)

The APT will tell you if there are any building preservation trusts in your area that could offer advice.

Architectural Heritage Fund (AHF)

The AHF can advise on all aspects of saving a listed building.

Own research

The local studies section of your library is likely to be a good source of information, as are books on local history and newspaper clippings. The internet is also an invaluable research tool on building types, industrial and commercial processes, and architectural characteristics that may help you better understand your building's history and function.

Approaching the owner

It is often said that there are no problem buildings, just problem owners. This may be an exaggeration, but it does indicate one of the biggest problems with buildings at risk. The future of many such buildings is jeopardised by owners who for a variety of reasons – ranging from neglect to lack of funds – have allowed their building to fall into disrepair. 'Problem' owners often refuse either to repair their buildings or sell them at a reasonable price to those with new uses in mind. These problems may be overcome, but the building will continue to deteriorate while negotiations take place.

It is always wise to find out the owner's intentions for the building before making an approach. If the owner intends to redevelop or sell the building, there may not be a role for your group. Alternatively, if the owner is co-operative but does not indicate a clear intention, there is a risk that your group will work hard to develop a proposal and investigate funding, only to find it has helped the owner to see the potential and sell the building elsewhere. If your work leads to a successful conservation and re-use then this must be seen as a positive outcome. In general, if the approach by your group is well informed and constructive the owner is more likely to seriously consider its merits. Access to the local authority's file on the building, which should include any planning application history, will give a good idea of the owner's real intentions. Bear in mind that they are likely to be quite different from yours!

Large historic buildings often attract a low valuation because of the extent and cost of necessary repairs. A building at risk will probably have been vacant or underused because it has not been economically viable for the owner to sell or rent it, or even do any necessary repair works. However, it might also be assumed that if the owner could have repaired and re-used a building, they would have done so. This may provide you with bargaining power when it comes to acquisition. The shortfall between the cost of repairing a building and the actual price that, once completed, it might secure on the market is known as the 'heritage deficit'. The public sector sources that private owners might seek to use to bridge this deficit are very limited. However, a charitable trust is eligible to seek funds from a wider [see Chapter 12] pool, such as the **Heritage Lottery Fund**. This is further explained in Chapter 12.

In the light of your expression of interest an owner may perceive that the value of the property is rising, especially as the approach is from the voluntary sector and holds promise of charitable funding. Should the owner continue let the building deteriorate, bear in mind that any perception of an increase in its value can be dampened by the local authority, which can warn owners of their statutory obligations to repair and maintain listed buildings. Councils are sometimes reluctant to use the heavy hand the law affords them but will often advise the owner about their maintenance responsibilities, which may be enough to persuade them to act. If a building is in real danger it is helpful to know the legal powers available to a local authority before you talk to the owner.

[see Chapter 7] Do make every attempt to be open with the owner and make clear your interest in the future of the building. They may be content for you to have access to the building and examine its condition as part of developing proposals for its conservation and re-use.

Even if the objectives of the owner are not the same as yours it may still pay to continue exploring the building's potential for re-use – especially if the current owner's plans are likely to damage the building (and may therefore be rejected by local authority planners). However, do not waste time trying to galvanise a plan for the building if the owner's plans are progressing in the right direction without you.

Salt Warehouse
and Number 4
Warehouse,
Sowerby Bridge
[case study p72]

The Planning Officer
Anytown District Council
Anytown

Dear Mr Smith

The Old Mill, Anytown

I am writing to you in relation to The Old Mill, a derelict historic industrial building in Anytown that has recently been included in English Heritage's Buildings at Risk Register. I have been a resident in Anytown for six years and in that period I have seen the building abandoned by its previous users, the Real Cotton Co., and fall into a state of dereliction through neglect.

The Old Mill is a valuable asset to the town of Anytown, contributing to its historic identity and beauty. With so much new development for housing, industry and retail occurring in and around the town, it seems that the opportunities to use existing resources and reduce unnecessary greenfield development should be taken.

I would like to explore the possibility of developing a community-led not-for-profit solution for the re-use of The Old Mill. I believe that the regeneration of this historic building could not only improve the quality of the town's built environment but provide facilities to address some of the social and economic needs of our community.

I am aware that the building's owner received planning permission in January 2002 to convert it to thirteen residences. As there does not appear to have been any action in relation to the listed buildings on the site, which are becoming increasingly vulnerable to irreparable damage, we would urge you to consider whether it is financially viable for the private sector to implement a project to save them.

In the absence of a robust private sector proposal it is sensible to consider alternative routes to secure the future of the listed building that can attract sufficient funding to bridge the conservation deficit. I would be very grateful if we could arrange to meet in order to discuss the future of this important building, so that we may start to consider how it may be saved for the benefit of the community.

Yours sincerely

2

GETTING TOGETHER A PARTNERSHIP

Having investigated and decided that a chosen building
has the potential to be developed as a voluntary-sector
project, **RTH** has found that the next step is to gather
together a group of like-minded and interested people
to take matters forward. The project will certainly be
more work than one or two people could manage.

Your group will benefit from being introduced in detail
to the project idea at the first meeting. Although several
members of the group are likely to be familiar with the
building, there will be others who know less. It is important
that everybody is briefed. A group visit, provided this does
not cause ill will on the owner's part, is desirable.

Suggested agenda for an initial meeting

1 Welcome and introductions

An opportunity to welcome any new members of the group.
Whoever chairs the meeting can explain that people have
been invited to attend to consider setting up a Partnership.

2 Ways ahead

Why work as a group? A project is more likely to be successful
if it has the support of a range of people and institutions willing
to contribute their time, expertise and influence. Given that
the project is for the benefit of its surrounding community,
local people are likely to be enthusiastic about being part of
its development.

Getting key organisations involved from the beginning is
vital and will help galvanise support and facilitate progress.

3 Further members

Who should be involved? Most importantly, **representatives of
local community organisations** will help develop a re-use

proposal that addresses community needs and helps foster a sense of 'ownership' among local people. A project is more likely to succeed if it has community support. If you do not already know how to contact community organisations, the local authority should be able to provide this information.

A local authority **Conservation Officer** or a representative of the **Planning** or **Economic Development Department**, or equivalent. The role and goodwill of a local authority is of fundamental importance. Try to secure as much officer and cross-party councillor support as possible. Councils exercise key statutory powers with regard to planning permission, building regulations and listed building consent (which is required for listed buildings in addition to normal planning permission). Local government support can provide wider political support and specialist know-how, and will lend credibility with funding and public agencies. Most local authorities will support the objectives of community-led projects and have an interest in conserving historic buildings.

Representatives from local charities and trusts, especially building preservation trusts and development trusts. Their experience of operating voluntary organisations to restore historic buildings will be invaluable. Contact the

[see Contacts]   Association of Preservation Trusts for information about building preservation trusts operating in your area.

Local business people, who have an understanding of local economic issues.

Well-known public figures can raise your group's profile and provide leverage, recognition and credibility.

A **strong independent chair** and **secretary** are absolutely invaluable, but don't worry if at the initial meeting there appear to be no obvious candidates for these posts. You can nominate people on a temporary basis and, hopefully, identify the right people later, once the nature and scope of the work is better understood.

In the course of developing your project, the group will probably need advice from specialist professionals. They need not necessarily be permanent group members but can be called in as needed:

Specialist heritage organisations, such as English Heritage, Historic Scotland, Cadw: Welsh Historic Monuments, or Environment and Heritage Service in Northern Ireland, and the relevant amenity and conservation organisations. They can provide specialist advice and insights on national heritage and conservation policies.

A **conservation architect**, who can help understand the elements of the building, its architectural and historic importance, and how these constrain what it can be used for. This is a professional who, in addition to a normal architectural qualification, has a qualification or specific experience in projects involving historic properties and will, therefore, understand the special issues involved in developing proposals for their sympathetic re-use. The Register of Architects Accredited in Building Conservation will provide details of registered architects knowledgeable in the conservation of historic buildings and demonstrating experience in this field. [www.aabc-register.co.uk]. If you cannot readily find someone, the **Royal Institute of British Architects (RIBA)** offers a scheme by [see Contacts] which you can access pro bono help from a suitable professional advisor. The **RIBA** can also help you identify suitable architectural practices to invite to tender for your contract work later on. A **building surveyor** with conservation experience would also be useful; the **Royal Institution of Chartered Surveyors (RICS)** will also provide advice. [www.rics.org]

A **lawyer**, who can advise on the various legal issues that must be addressed in structuring the organisation to implement the project and the contractual arrangements to be made. An enthusiastic generalist solicitor would help, but, ideally, you need someone with experience of charity law.

An **accountant** or **bank official**, who can provide skills to manage the project's finances. Someone with experience in funding community initiatives would be especially useful.

Depending on your project, other project-specific factors, such as ecological, archaeological, environmental, political, curatorial, and visitor management issues, may also need to be addressed. Do bear in mind these issues when approaching people to serve on the group. It will take time to assemble the range of people you need, so don't panic if you start off with gaps. A good project will attract the expertise you seek.

4 Discussion

What should be discussed? It will take time for all the issues relating to the building and its potential re-use to come to the surface, so do not expect to solve all its problems at the first meeting. The real objective at the first meeting is to establish as much common ground as possible. This will bind the group and serve to remind you why you became involved. RTH has found that initial meetings are an opportunity for different parties to express their views and discuss options for the building's future. Structuring this process as a brainstorming session on certain key themes may help:

— What condition is the building in?
— Is the local authority likely to have to exercise its powers to protect the building in the short-term?
— What is the building and site's architectural and historic importance?
— What statutory designations apply to the building and site?
— What information does the local authority have about the owner's intentions?
— What are the building's prospects? Are they likely to improve markedly without your group's intervention?
— Does the local community have particular social, environmental or economic needs? Are these reflected in any national or European initiatives for the area?
— What personal associations does the building have for local people?
— What are the site's proposed future uses, as designated in the statutory Local Plan?
— In what way would the building's re-use benefit the local community?
— Are there any known contamination issues relating to the site?
— Are there any known ecological or archaeological issues relating to the site?

The first meeting will probably reveal that the group lacks expertise in some specialist areas. Don't worry about this. You should start to think about how to address the gaps, but there is plenty of time to find the right people. The size of the team will depend on the potential complexity of the project: too few and it may not include all the required skills, or lack momentum; too many and discussions will become prolonged, hampering progress. Bear in mind that some people may be happy to give informal advice but may, for personal or professional reasons, decline to become members, although they may still contribute to discussions as observers. As meetings progress the group's strengths and weaknesses will become apparent. Undertaking or commissioning appropriate research, or inviting suitably skilled people to join, can bridge any areas of weakness.

5 Resolve to set up a Partnership

Voluntary groupings can become paralysed by arguments about who is entitled to attend or vote, and without clear decision-making procedures it may be tempting to re-visit issues that have already been resolved, perhaps because a new member has joined. Without an agreed and representative membership, factions can also hijack discussions.

Therefore, the meeting should include a resolution to establish a representative **Partnership** to take responsibility for developing the project. The project will take time to implement and a Partnership sets the group on a semi-formal footing, which helps to ensure that people who have agreed to contribute take it seriously and work according to agreed rules.

The existence of a Partnership also provides proper accountability and gives the project credibility: an organised group will carry more weight with local authorities, regional development agencies and other significant bodies.

A Partnership **Memorandum of Understanding** sets out the organisations and individuals who are entitled to attend and vote, and objectives, terms of reference and other procedures for conducting business. *This is not a legally binding structure*.

A model Memorandum of Understanding, which can be amended to suit different circumstances, is included at the end of this chapter. It offers good rules of engagement.

Regular round-table meetings will help the Partnership share information and understanding, and contribute to its capacity to work together towards a viable re-use strategy. In the early days the Partnership may disagree about the form of the final project but constructive discussion at regular meetings will help. Projects involving the repair of historic buildings invariably take time to come to fruition. Take care not to overload willing individuals with work, and be prepared for periods when intense commitment is required.

6 Date for the next meeting

It is important to set diary dates to maintain momentum.

As the Partnership is likely to be working together for a number of years it makes sense to establish it on a formal footing. This does not have to be a legally-binding structure. A Partnership Memorandum of Understanding sets out the organisation's objectives and serves to formalise terms of reference and working arrangements. This is sufficient to enable the project to get off the ground, engage in formal negotiations, and protect it from being dominated or hijacked by factions.

The [insert the name of your building here] **Partnership Memorandum of Understanding**

The Partnership Group ('The Partnership') represents the bodies and organisations ('The Partnership Members') referred to in Appendix A.

A. The Partnership wishes to record its intentions regarding its joint participation in encouraging the private, voluntary and public sectors to work together with the common purpose of regenerating [insert the name of your building here], [insert the name of your town or region here]. The relevant area is shown edged red on the attached plan, which is part of the administrative area of the Council [insert the name of your local authority].

B. The Partnership wishes to record in this Understanding details of the constitution, terms of reference and working arrangements it has adopted.

C. Mission Statement
    'The Partnership has been established to protect and enhance the historical and environmental fabric of the [insert the name of your building here] *; to restore both the listed building's structure and associated buildings, to provide visitor access, to present an appropriate level of historical interpretation, create appropriate new uses and business opportunities; and to assist sustainable regeneration of the area within which the building is located.'*

16

1 Objectives of Understanding

The Partnership will collaborate to process the following objectives in the first instance:

1.1 To promote the conservation of the heritage and respect the distinctive quality of the listed structures and buildings of the [insert the name of your building here] and to promote appropriate regeneration and development in the adjoining area.

1.2 To work together to develop the vision and strategy for the early implementation of this regeneration initiative.

1.3 To develop a project that will refurbish the building's area as a prosperous, vibrant, safe and accessible work place and visitor destination, providing employment in a high quality environment.

1.4 To promote the project actively and to work together to obtain funding for its implementation.

1.5 To help raise civic pride and promote an image demonstrating the location as a sound investment opportunity for new uses that will aid sustainable regeneration.

1.6 To develop community involvement in the regeneration of the building.

2 Terms of the Agreement

2.1 The Partnership intends that this Understanding should last for an initial period of three years from the date hereof but may be continued thereafter until terminated in accordance with clause 2.2.

2.2 This Understanding can be terminated after the initial three-year period, at any time, by a Partnership Member giving not less than three months' notice of their intention to terminate.

3 Terms of Reference

The aims and purpose of the Partnership are set out as follows:

3.1 To endorse and agree the details of the bids to funding bodies for the refurbishment of the building and any other associated conservation and regeneration proposals.

3.2 To oversee the implementation of the funded works and review progress.

3.3 To endorse and agree the details of any further proposals that conserve and regenerate the area of the building.

3.4 To act as a consultative group to discuss future policies and developments that may affect the area within which the building is located and provide comments or advice as required.

4 Constitution and Working Arrangements of the Partnership

4.1 The Partnership shall consist of ten Members and be representative of organisations, property interests and businesses, each with a commitment to the furtherance of the objectives stated in this Understanding.

4.2 Each Partnership Member shall have one vote.

4.3 The Chair and the Deputy Chair of the Partnership shall be elected by the majority vote of the Partnership Members present at a meeting convened under Clause 5.2 below. The Chair and Deputy Chair shall not belong to the same organisation.

4.4 The Chair and Deputy Chair shall have a fixed term of office for the initial three-year period. At the end of that term an election will be held for a new Chair and Deputy Chair. The previous Chair and Deputy Chair shall be eligible for re-election at a meeting convened under Clause 5.2.

4.5 If the Chair or Deputy Chair of the Partnership resigns or otherwise leaves the Partnership before their term has ended an election will take place at a meeting convened under Clause 5.2 to appoint replacements.

4.6 The Chair shall have the casting vote should the need arise.

4.7 At a meeting where the Chair and Deputy Chair are not present, the meeting shall elect by majority vote a Chair from the Members present for the meeting only.

4.8 Partnership Members shall be entitled to nominate an individual to be a substitute at meetings which the Member is unable to attend. The nominated representative at such meetings shall be able to vote on behalf of the absent Member. The list of nominated representatives will be maintained by [eg the name of your local authority].

4.9 If a Partnership Member resigns or otherwise leaves the Partnership then the Chair, Deputy Chair and other Members are required to ensure that no fewer than four Members participate in the decision and shall be empowered to appoint a new Member to the Partnership.

4.10 Subject to Clauses 4.12, 4.13, 4.14 below decisions are taken by a majority vote.

4.11 Council Officers and others may attend meetings, upon invitation, as advisers but will not be entitled to vote.

4.12 The Partnership may terminate the Membership of any Partnership Member, or their substitute, provided that such a person shall have the right to be heard by the Partnership before a final decision is taken and that any decision has a vote of 75% of the Partnership in favour of termination.

4.13 The Partnership may amend or alter its constitution, terms of reference and working arrangements provided that any decision to do so has a vote of 75% of the Partnership in favour.

4.14 The Partnership may terminate this Understanding in accordance with the provisions in Clause 2.2 above, provided that any decision to do so has a vote of 75% of the Partnership in favour.

4.15 No more than 20% of the representatives of the Partnership may consist of members of the Local Authority.

5 Meetings of the Group

5.1 The Partnership will meet not less than twice a year or as necessary and a report evaluating progress will be submitted to the Partnership Members twice a year. No fewer than seven days' notice in writing of a meeting will be given to Members.

5.2 A quorum of the Partnership shall consist of at least four representatives who shall each be from a different Partnership Member.

5.3 A special meeting of the Partnership may be called at any time by the Chair, or by any two Members, of which no fewer than four days' notice in writing shall be given to other Members of the matters to be discussed.

6 Sub-Groups

6.1 Sub-Groups of the Partnership may be established (if necessary, but should be kept to a minimum) to conduct specific/specialised tasks.

6.2 Sub-Groups will normally not exceed six Members and the Chair of the Sub-Group must be appointed by the Partnership. Members of a Sub-Group may be appointed who are not Members of the Partnership.

6.3 Chairs of Sub-Groups will work under the direction of the Partnership, which will determine the terms of reference, powers, duration and composition and will report back to the Partnership.

7 Members' Personal Interests

7.1 It shall be the duty of every representative of the Partnership to disclose any personal interest in matters coming before the Partnership and, in the event of a conflict of interest, shall at the discretion of the meeting withdraw from voting on the matter, or withdraw from the meeting whilst the matter is under discussion.

8 Powers

In furtherance of the objectives set out earlier the Partnership may exercise the following powers:

8.1 The Partnership may jointly submit funding applications or other applications in support of the project, or bid under the aegis of one organisation on behalf of the Partnership, and invite and receive contributions provided that in raising funds the parties shall not undertake any substantial permanent trading activities and shall conform to any relevant requirements.

8.2 The Partnership may cooperate with other organisations, voluntary bodies and statutory authorities operating in furtherance of the objects set out in Clause 1 or of similar purposes and to exchange information and advice with them.

8.3 The Partnership may together appoint and constitute such Sub-Groups as it thinks fit.

8.4 The Partnership may do such other lawful things as are necessary for the achievement of the objectives set out in Clause 1 above.

9 Administration, Accounts, Receipts and Expenditure

9.1 [e.g. the name of your local authority or other agency] undertakes to provide administrative support for the meeting arrangement, agendas, minute taking, circulation of papers and to retain the list of nominated representatives as detailed in 4.8 above.

9.2 No member organisation shall be obliged to underwrite any shortfall of income against expenditure.

10 Confidentiality

The members of the Partnership hereby agree that they will treat all information supplied by one to the other as unrestricted unless there are exceptional circumstances. Where there are items of a confidential nature they shall be marked as confidential on agenda papers and treated as totally confidential by the parties (including all those instructed by the Partnership). The parties shall not reveal the confidential information at any time to any outside parties without the prior consent of the parties (except to the extent which may be necessary to carry out objectives set out in Clause 1 above).

11 Ownership of Documents

The Partnership hereby declares that it will be the terms of the appointment of any external professional advisers to the Partnership that all plans, specifications, reports and other documents provided for use by the Partnership will become the property of the Partnership unless otherwise specified.

12 General

12.1 To avoid doubt it is expressly confirmed by all parties that this Understanding is not intended to be legally binding between the parties or constitute a legal partnership.

12.2 It is further agreed by all parties that the incurring of expenditure by or on behalf of any of the parties will not be deemed to imply the establishment of a legal partnership or a legally binding obligation between the parties.

12.3 For the avoidance of doubt the Partnership agrees, by entering into this Understanding, that the Members of the Partnership will neither collectively nor individually assume any financial liability in connection with work undertaken by the Partnership.

12.4 [The name of your local authority] 's participation in this Partnership is without prejudice to its role as Local Planning Authority and Highways Authority and to the need to adhere to statutory regulations.

12.5 [The name of your local authority] accepts no liability for any professional advice offered by its representatives.

[date]

[Signed by the Members of the Group]

Each Member may nominate a substitute to vote at meetings at which the Member is unable to attend according to Clause 4.8. Other interested parties may be invited to meetings but may not have voting rights according to Clause 4.11.

3

FINDING COMMON GROUND

The new Partnership exists only because of a common interest in a building. The first Partnership meeting should, therefore, clarify the Partnership's common objectives, bind members into the venture and convey a purposeful and business-like approach to the task.

The first objective should be to raise awareness and understanding of the importance of the building, its history, architecture and place in the community, and the reasons for saving it. People may think that they 'know' the building, particularly if it is prominent in the townscape, but it is likely that few will really appreciate all its aspects. It is essential that everyone understands the value of the building if the Partnership is to do justice to the task of restoring it.

Do prepare carefully for this first meeting, using an agenda to tackle your goals. Depending on the project's specifics the Partnership may wish to discuss issues in a different order, with some matters requiring more than one Partnership meeting.

Suggested agenda for Partnership meeting 1

1 Welcome and introductions
An opportunity to welcome everyone to the meeting, explain its purpose and outline the order of business. Those present should introduce themselves and their interest in the building. This is important as people may be meeting others for the first time.

2 Appointment of Chair and Vice-Chair
As this is the Partnership's first meeting it may be sensible to appoint a temporary **Chair**. A permanent Chair and **Vice-Chair** can be appointed when things settle down. Appoint a **Secretary** to take minutes and be responsible for official

Partnership correspondence, but make sure this is someone reliable who has access to administrative back-up if necessary.

3 Why the building should be saved

It is a good idea to open with some presentations on the importance of the building and the reasons for saving it. This is an opportunity to inspire members about the value of the building and focus on what needs to be done to conserve and re-use it. For example, you could ask the local authority's **Conservation** or **Planning Officer**, or a local historian, to talk about the building's architectural and historic importance, preferably using some visuals. Community representatives might also discuss local attitudes towards the building.

Speakers should cover:
— The location of the building
— The history of the building and its local significance
— The importance of the building's architecture, including the statutory protection it enjoys e.g. listed or in a conservation area
— The building's present condition and any security problems
— Past and any current proposals for the building
— Planning policy towards the building – is it included in the local plan?
— Known development issues
— Access issues
— Environmental issues e.g. contamination caused by previous use
— The views of the owner if known

Presentations may be followed by a 'Questions and Answers' discussion, providing an opportunity to consider any of the major issues arising. For example, the owner may have inappropriate plans for the building, or the local authority may need to be encouraged to take statutory action to prevent further deterioration. Action points from this discussion should be allocated to willing Members.

4 Briefing document

The Partnership will find it useful to have a briefing document that describes the building, the reasons for creating the

Partnership and its objectives. This will summarise different issues affecting the building and act as a useful reference tool for Members and interested parties. It will also be helpful when briefing consultants later on. The Member(s) tasked with writing the document can use notes from the earlier speakers and supplement these with further research.

5 Agreement

Those assembled should agree to set a deadline to sign the Partnership **Memorandum of Understanding**, indicating their commitment to developing a solution for the building. Partnership Members should sign and return their copies as soon as possible, or, if they represent an organisation, obtain its assent. Representatives of some organisations may not be able to become fully-fledged Members but may be willing to attend meetings as observers. If Members feel the Partnership could benefit from the skills of others, now is the time to agree whom to approach.

6 Any other business

An opportunity to raise any issues not already covered. Avoid debate about 'big issues' at this stage, such as future new uses for the building.

7 Date of next meeting

Agree the date of the next meeting, which should depend on the urgency with which Members are prepared to address the task. Four to six weeks may be considered a reasonable interval for Members to tackle their specific action points. Try also to agree dates for several future meetings in advance, or agree to meet on a certain day in the month; the sooner a programme of meetings is established, the better. The Chair may also remind Members to sign and return their Memorandum of Understanding, and tackle their action points with gusto!

Lomeshaye Bridge Mill, Nelson, Lancashire [case study]

Lomeshaye Bridge Mill is located in the Whitefield area of Nelson, one of the few remaining 'cotton towns' of the 19th century, which retains a rare collection of housing, industrial, commercial and community buildings. The Mill fronts the Leeds and Liverpool canal. Parts of Whitefield were proposed for housing demolition which would have left the Mill and its weaving sheds isolated on the edge of a new build community. The demolition proposals were overturned, largely in light of resident opposition, and the community then addressed how best the area might be renewed in a heritage-led regeneration initiative.

The Mill and Weaving Sheds are owned by the Heritage Trust for the North West (HTNW) and are recognised as a key part of the wider renewal and regeneration strategy for Whitefield.

With RTH advice key stakeholders in the community held a Planning Day to consider the options. It concluded that, with so much housing proposed to be refurbished, the need was for economic and social facilities. The Planning Day discussed the existing economic characteristics of the community, known skill levels, unemployment, and aspirations for jobs. The likely cost of refurbishing the building, and the consequent impact on rent levels, was taken into account and comparisons made with existing available floor space. A briefing was provided on the likely funding regimes that might be drawn upon for the capital needed.

The Mill's location alongside the canal, and the potential to attract canal boat users and other visitors using the towpaths, as well as the potential to create a major 'destination' in a regenerated heritage area, were seen as important opportunities.

The Planning Day agreed a strategy to use the Mill for craft/hi-tech small businesses attractive to the qualified school leavers and young people who would otherwise have to commute long distances for work. The ground floor was proposed for community space/gallery and a café for local people and a 'destination' for canal boat users and towpath walkers. The adjoining Weaving Sheds were proposed for small business use, especially those involved in traditional building skills. An Advisory Group (Partnership) was established to carry forward these proposals.

Meanwhile, the regeneration of Whitefield was subject to a week-long Enquiry by Design exercise that involved the key organisations and funding agencies. The proposals for the Mill were judged to be a 'quick win' for the strategy and endorsed as meeting community needs. A Development Brief has been prepared by the HTNW with RTH and submitted for Townscape Heritage Initiative funding.

4

CEMENTING PROGRESS: LOOKING AT NEW USES

The first meeting will have clarified the building's importance, set up the Partnership, and expressed its Members' intention to pursue the building's conservation and re-use. Now is the time to examine in more detail the needs of the community and how a restored building can contribute to fulfilling them. Please remember this health warning: depending on the size and complexity of your project you may take longer (or less time) to address the items of business **RTH** has suggested for Partnership meetings. This Handbook is a suggested programme of decision-making, but all projects are different and involve unique situations that cannot always be predicted. So it is only a route map to keep you moving in the right direction.

Suggested agenda for Partnership meeting 2

1 Welcome and any further introductions
An opportunity to welcome any new Members of the Partnership.

2 Notes of previous meeting
Agree the minutes and ask Members who were assigned action points at the last meeting to report on progress. Avoid revisiting issues that have already been agreed.

3 Partnership announcement
All Members should have signed and returned the Memorandum of Understanding. New Members should be invited to do this as soon as possible. Agree if it would be appropriate to issue a press statement about the new Partnership and its objectives, bearing in mind the attitude of the owner.

4 Social, economic and strategic context of the building
Many voluntary organisations concerned with regenerating historic buildings want the new uses it will accommodate to

address the needs of their communities. It is essential that you engage in a constructive dialogue with a wide range of community-based organisations in your area to identify opportunities for your project to help meet community needs.

It will help pinpoint community strengths, weaknesses, opportunities and threats if you invite representatives from the council's economic development team, the Chamber of Commerce and any local organisations concerned with employment, training and social issues to talk to you about how these might be addressed in the re-used building. This will help you understand local economic conditions, including existing commercial rents and the likely demand for space in your building. If there is high unemployment in your area you must be realistic about the chances of creating new businesses or attracting existing ones to rent space, and the kinds of rent levels you can expect to obtain. You need a fairly hard-headed assessment of local economic conditions and any regeneration or development opportunities in your area.

The following might be discussed:
— Size of the local population
— Strategic location of the site in relation to other centres of population
— Unemployment levels in the local community
— Strengths and weaknesses of the local economy and main employment activities
— Local commercial rent levels and demand for rented space
— Potential to create new businesses
— Plans for regeneration or development in the area
— How the site might contribute to tourism in the area and its likely fit with the existing tourism infrastructure
— Social and economic objectives of the local authority
— Lack of skilled employment (prompting low wage issues etc)
— Social problems particular to the area e.g. lack of local skills, training and education
— Levels of local literacy and numeracy
— Availability of local recreational and leisure facilities
— Availability of community resources, such as meeting spaces

Speakers should address regional or national economic and regeneration policies, as well as initiatives affecting the local area. They should be able to explain to which programmes the Partnership is eligible to apply for funding. Economic development officers will also know about any funding programmes specifically designed to address economic and social difficulties in your area.

Socio-economic data is also available from the census online **www.neighbourhood.statistics.gov.uk**, and from local Chambers of Commerce. Contact Regional Development Agencies and regeneration bodies, but remember that these are called different things in different parts of the UK. You can

[see Contacts]

invite one of these organisations to provide a speaker for your meeting.

A good understanding of the character of your local area, its people and their needs is vital to developing a project that is genuinely useful and sustainable in the long term. If there is no local demand for rented floor space there is no point in primarily re-using your building for this purpose! If the Partnership understands what is needed locally, and why, it will enable it to talk knowledgeably to funding bodies and other stakeholders about the contribution the project could make.

A good understanding of how the project may relate to other businesses in the area will help the Partnership identify potential sources of funding and co-operation. Viable re-use proposals may also emerge from these discussions, which will help prepare the ground for a feasibility study and the development of a future business plan.

5 Discussion and SWOT analysis

Following the presentations the Partnership can discuss the issues raised. One way of structuring this is for Partnership Members to divide the points raised into categories of

[see overleaf]

strengths, weaknesses, opportunities and threats (SWOT).

6 New uses

The process of a SWOT analysis will enable the Partnership to discuss the advantages and disadvantages of a wide range of potential uses. Using this method you can eliminate the least likely proposals and move forward with the more favoured new uses. A long-list of realistic possibilities can be drawn up. Now is not the time to decide on final uses – the process of sifting and further elimination will come later.

Bear in mind that just because the Partnership is interested in the future of its building does not automatically mean that it

Example of SWOT analysis

Strengths	Weaknesses	Opportunities	Threats
The local population is motivated and organised through community organisations.	Community groups may prefer to use multiple different meeting venues, as at present.	A crafts training centre on the site will provide a stream of crafts-people who need affordable premises in which to work.	The affordable work-shops may be over-reliant on the training programme. If the programme fails, the workshops may do also.
There are a number of similar heritage attractions nearby, so tourists are already being attracted to the area.	If the project takes too long to develop, community groups could lose momentum and disband.	An opportunity exists to link up with existing local heritage sites in the area e.g. single tickets for multiple venues. (The project will be competing with other heritage attractions and may not attract sufficient visitors.)	Estate agents indicate that they do not receive many inquiries for affordable accommodation from business start-ups.
The building provides ample space to accommodate business start-ups, charging affordable rents.	The site had quite a specific historic use, so may appeal to fewer visitors than other historic buildings.		

has to be the vehicle that completes the task. The Partnership may just develop the 'vision' for the regeneration project, indicating how it could be financially viable, and an existing charitable or private organisation may be willing to implement your proposals. The appropriate mechanism for restoring a building may ultimately be a Trust established for the purpose; an existing charity; a private company; or a mixture of all these. It is possible that notifying people of the Partnership's plans will be enough to spark private sector interest. The point is, do not feel you have to temper your ideas about the building's future simply because you think the Partnership may not be able to carry them out under its own steam. See the section below for further information on new uses.

7 Briefing document

As for your Partnership's first meeting, ensure that the knowledge gained from the economics-driven and community-driven presentations is recorded in a briefing document and circulated.

8 Any other business

9 Date of next meeting

New uses to consider

In deciding which uses the Partnership wants to investigate further, and which to omit, you risk losing some supporters. However, experience suggests that saying 'no' at an early stage to non-compatible uses is essential. Inappropriate uses, or mixes of uses, can drive out better ones and undermine the long-term credibility of the project.

It is a good idea to see if you can identify which parts of your building might best suit particular uses. Try to avoid allowing any potential key revenue-producing tenant to have first choice of space; they usually want the most accessible prime space, which leaves you with the less attractive or inaccessible parts. It is also important to bear in mind that space used by the public needs to be near the main entrance; again this is usually where the key tenant would like to be.

While a 24-hour building is probably not desirable RTH's experience is that daytime-only activities are less likely to be viable and are not as appealing as those that attract people in the evenings and at weekends. Even if these uses require that part of the building be closed off, they create an occupied and busy environment attractive to the local community and provide increased security for tenants. Mixed-use is also, in many cases, the best way to achieve economic viability. However, bear in mind that if you include a residential element you will need to avoid other uses that may cause conflict with residents, such as a noisy bar or restaurant. Getting the mix of uses right can be tricky.

There are advantages and disadvantages to a broad range of potential uses:

Housing

Many large mills, warehouses and other industrial buildings have been successfully converted for residential use – and not just for fashionable loft living. Demand for urban-style housing, for both sale and rent, shows little sign of diminishing and could be incorporated into a mixed-use scheme. In an area in need of housing a residential component might provide financial viability and bring '24-hour' life to the building.

A degree of compatibility with other uses is obviously essential. The Partnership could consider housing for sale, shared-ownership housing or housing for rent: talk to both private housing developers and local housing associations before proceeding. You also need to be certain that the building can be successfully converted to housing without seriously detracting from its intrinsic character. Large open floor plates, for example in mills, might be best left like that, as subdivision may damage their architectural value or require awkward-shaped domestic rooms.

Workshops and offices

Projects often contain space for workshops and offices as these can ensure a reliable income if rented to a number of different commercial organisations and individuals. Apart from live/work units, commercial activities are best located together in one part of the building, separate from any social provision, and must have security arrangements. Buildings can be sub-divided and fitted-out to a range of standards depending on user requirements. Community groups sometimes favour managed workspace, which offers affordable, small-scale, mixed-use commercial and workshop accommodation. This is most suited to small or start-up businesses, which create local employment, and usually only works if there is sufficient scale.

Historic industrial buildings can offer enormous scope for flexible commercial floor-space. The large floor plates are particularly suited to the needs of modern open-plan offices, and many hi-tech and high-value companies have successfully located in former industrial buildings. Small workshop units or affordable workspace for craft industries also fit well.

Cultural facilities

Communities often require flexible spaces for meetings, performances and exhibitions. These, together with art and retail workshops and art galleries, will help attract visitors and provide a stream of customers for cafés and bars. Increasingly, 'cultural industries' are recognised as drivers for economic growth and are often attracted to regenerated landmark historic buildings. Cultural businesses can take advantage of the excitement and interest created by the co-operative atmosphere that can develop when creative projects locate together. Space could be allocated for local artists, giving them valuable exposure to potential markets.

Heritage-related facilities

Local communities often like to see part of the building reserved for a display related to its original use. However, this can be costly to establish, maintain and update, and may not attract regular visitors for very long. However, display and interpretation information and artefacts can be integrated with other uses, such as cafés, but are unlikely to be sustainable on their own.

Conference or meeting rooms

Converted historic buildings can offer excellent opportunities for unusual conference or commercial meeting rooms, particularly if there are good catering facilities in the building or nearby, and good transport links. There is growing demand for this type of accommodation, especially from business agencies, local authorities and educational establishments.

Restaurants and bars

Historic buildings are often ideal for restaurants and bars, which work well in an unusual environment. Sensitively located, they can be useful facilities to have in a building with other users, who will be a good source of custom, and provide a meeting place for everyone in the building.

Leisure uses

Large floor plates make some buildings easy to convert for leisure uses, such as fitness centres. Successful schemes have included swimming pools, squash and badminton courts, fencing, judo, boxing, dancing classes, roller-skating, table tennis, games room, pool and snooker tables, bowling alleys, cinemas, night clubs and internet cafés.

Community facilities

If the community needs educational facilities, consider making space for local training and education providers. Talk to your local Education Authority and colleges. Your building might be ideal for an outreach campus or could accommodate a branch of the local library, a community centre, youth club, nursery or playgroup.

Shopping facilities

If your building is likely to attract large numbers of visitors there may be opportunities for unusual or bespoke retail outlets.

Navigation Warehouse (Calder & Hebble), Wakefield [case study]

Navigation Warehouse is a Grade II* Listed 18th-century riverside grain warehouse in Wakefield that had lain vacant for over 20 years. It was in an area of decline surrounded by mills, some in use for their original purpose and others in a mix of economic uses or vacant.

The Partnership established by RTH was determined to bring the Warehouse back into use and, initially, agreed that it should be the location for the display of works by Wakefield sculptor Barbara Hepworth. It wanted to see what lessons could be learned from projects involving the adaptation of complex historic buildings, and to investigate the potential for heritage-led regeneration in waterside locations.

The Partnership visited the canal system in Birmingham, where the previously neglected canals had been reopened as the centre-piece of a large private sector scheme involving offices, residential, restaurants and pubs, and other facilities, and the regenerated docks at Bristol and Gloucester. These visits confirmed that waterways are effective catalysts for regeneration and that heritage buildings offer real prospects for quality schemes. They also provided warnings about the dangers of poor quality architecture for new buildings in sensitive heritage locations.

The tour included a visit to the Great Western Railway Works in Swindon, the former railway works that has, by clever and imaginative design, been converted for use as a shopping centre while retaining the core of its original character and architectural features. This showed that the most unlikely buildings could be adapted for new uses. A visit to the Custard Factory in Birmingham, now home to an eclectic mix of new businesses in the arts, culture and media sector, demonstrated how new uses can be mixed to form a creative hub of mutually supportive economic activities, and how cultural activities can be an economic driver.

These visits raised the Partnership's ambitions for a quality project at Navigation Warehouse as a catalyst for a wider waterfront regeneration with emphasis on cultural and recreational/visitor businesses. The City Council supported this vision and designated the waterfront as a Conservation Area; and the other industrial buildings were Listed. A masterplan, now being implemented, was devised for the Waterfront based on bringing Hepworth's work to Wakefield.

It was eventually decided that the Hepworth Collection would be better housed in a larger building but the recognition of the importance of good design was reflected in an International Architectural Competition for a new gallery. The Warehouse will be used instead for office and public purposes.

5

SHARING EXPERTISE: STUDY VISITS

With a good background knowledge of its building and the issues affecting it, the Partnership should be thinking creatively about its re-use. This part of project development is fun: be open-minded and try not to hold on to preconceived ideas of how the building should be re-used. If the building is anything but very small, expect to develop an innovative mixed-use solution.

In RTH's experience a study visit to a number of completed regeneration projects is an excellent way of raising a Partnership's aspirations and inspiring it with creative re-use possibilities. People who have been through the process, including private sector entrepreneurs, developers and other community groups, are usually only too happy to talk about their experience and how they arrived at their building's cocktail of uses. 'Seeing is believing' when it comes to heritage re-use – prepare to be surprised by how apparently problematic buildings turn into excellent spaces for contemporary functions. Sometimes the more unusual or problematic the structure, the more interesting its re-use. For instance, at Mistley Quayside Maltings in Essex, awkwardly-shaped kilns and drying floors originally used to dry germinating barley are being converted into a restaurant, art gallery, meeting space and apartments.

Suggested agenda for Partnership meeting 3

1 Welcome

2 Notes of previous meeting
Agree the minutes and ask Members who were assigned action points at the last meeting to report on progress. Avoid revisiting issues that have already been agreed.

3 Study visit to exemplar projects

Ask members to suggest possible projects to visit. If you are struggling to find a suitable project to visit then building preservation trusts, or the local and national heritage organisations, are a good source of information.

RTH strongly recommends that Partnerships visit projects involving comparable historic buildings and socio-economic contexts. They should also include some of the uses the Partnership has in mind so that members can see for themselves what works well and what presents unforeseen difficulties. Lastly, try to cut down travelling time and cost by selecting projects nearby. Undertaking a longer two-day study tour involving visits to geographically disparate groups of buildings will depend on the ability of Partnership members to find the time and funding.

Once you have a short-list of possible projects and dates for the visit a member of the Partnership should be given the task of writing to the projects to request a visit, explaining the reasons and requesting a tour from someone closely involved in the restoration process.

4 Briefing document

Would it be helpful for a member of the Partnership to write a briefing document, or a series of points on the findings of the study visit?

5 Any other business

6 Date of next meeting

Birnbeck Pier, built in 1867 linking Weston-super-Mare to Birnbeck Island.
[case study p60]

6

LOCAL CONSULTATION

The interests and views of the community are crucial. Most local people are likely to be familiar with the building and have a view about what should happen to it. If the Partnership has not done so already it should seek out local views and ideas. These may reaffirm the Partnership's thinking or yield fresh perspectives. It is desirable that local people see the conserved building as being relevant to their needs and as promoting local interests: it is hard to justify spending public money on a regeneration project that fails to achieve local endorsement.

Community Planning Day

RTH recommends a **Planning Day** as the best way to ensure that the Partnership engages the local community and key stakeholders. A Planning Day requires the Partnership to present its thoughts on the building, the issues affecting it and its potential for re-use to a wider audience. The idea of this one- or two-day event is to invite comments and discussion that will contribute to the development of a sensitive and appropriate proposal which reflects the objectives of a broad range of people. Involving local businesses, funding organisations and civic bodies at this formative stage also locks them into the process of project development, enables them to contribute and feel a sense of ownership, and ensures that they are 'primed' for subsequent stages when you will need their co-operation and support.

Useful contributors to a Planning Day may include representatives from:
— Community organisations
— Civic organisations
— Neighbouring properties
— Local businesses
— Heritage organisations

— Local councils
— Current owner or users of the building
— Successful heritage regeneration projects
— Potential funding bodies, if only as observers

The broader the range of people invited the better. They should receive, preferably in advance, an information pack, including photographs, a description of the building and its location, general information on socio-economic issues affecting the surrounding community, and the menu of suggested possibilities for new uses favoured by the Partnership.

If the Partnership has already developed its thoughts sufficiently it may be useful to produce a document outlining its understanding of the main issues. This will give delegates something to react to. The point of the Planning Day is to be receptive to new ideas and take into account the full spectrum of community views on the building before making a final choice of preferred uses.

The Partnership will need to host this event, and this will involve finding a date and venue that suits most people, sending out invitations and arranging mundane matters such as catering and the provision of notepads, flipcharts, pens etc. RTH has found that an independent facilitator can be helpful. If you use one, make sure you brief them well and that they are really independent.

Try to keep these questions in mind:
— What does the building mean to the community?
— What is happening to the building?
— What must be achieved to provide the building with a viable use?
— Who needs to be involved, and what needs to be discussed?
— What must be done with the results?
— What is the community's vision for the building?

The Partnership will have its own preferences, which should be expressed in some detail, but it is almost certain that the final proposals will be for a mix of uses, reflecting the capacity of the building. A combination of commercial and not-for-profit uses will enable the Partnership to draw on a range of funding sources while also creating a revenue stream. Most importantly, it will also allow you to address local aspirations. If you are to secure funding your completed project must be sustainable over the long-term, and generate sufficient income both to maintain the conserved building and meet operating costs.

Suggested agenda for a Planning Day

1 Welcome and introductions
Don't assume that everyone is known to everyone else.

2 The Partnership Approach
Describe the value of everyone working together to achieve a common aim.

3 How the Partnership became involved with the building
The Chair of the Partnership should describe how it came into being and how the project will be taken forward.

4 The building
Remember that some people may not be familiar with the building so it will be helpful to have some illustrations showing its character and potential.

5 The community's social and economic issues
Describe the main problems confronting your community and how the project might help to address these.

6 Re-use proposals
This is an opportunity for various interest groups to give their opinions. For example, community groups could describe the facilities that are needed, or a business representative could talk about the potential to create employment. New suggested uses should be added to the 'long list' of possible future uses that the Partnership already has.

7 Break (lunch and viewing of display material)

8 Workshop
RTH has found it useful to divide up delegates into groups of around 6 – 10 people and ask them to spend about 45 minutes discussing the following questions:
— Are the re-use proposals for the site sound? What issues arise from them?
— What other uses could be considered appropriate for the building?
— What do you think the project could bring to the area?

9   Discussion and prioritisation of issues identified, followed
    by closing remarks from the Chair

In putting together a final package of suggested uses, you
should discuss the following:

— Opportunities and limitations of the building and site: any
  conflicts between proposed uses, statutory requirements
  and the historic fabric. A conservation architect or surveyor
  will be able to advise the Partnership about those uses
  most suited to particular parts of the building and those
  which are not.

— Characteristics of the local economy: matching priorities
  to local problems and opportunities. Your local authority's
  economic development team and/or local business
  representatives will be able to steer discussion towards
  uses for which there is an identified local demand and,
  perhaps, suggest potential stakeholders.

Ongoing consultation
As the project develops it is essential to provide the
community, and especially those who attended the Planning
Day, with regular information. This could include a newsletter,
articles in the local press, exhibitions, public meetings, open
days and surveys. If it is possible you might attach signboards
to the building stating what you're doing – this shows the local
community that something is happening. The following may
also be considered:

— *Partnership community representation*
  It will strengthen the credibility of the Partnership with
  the local community if it contains at least one experienced
  community leader, for example from a local community or
  residents' association, or an established civic organisation.

— *Participation in meetings of local organisations*
  Members of the Partnership who are active in other local
  organisations should undertake to report on the project's
  progress. Do reach out to other organisations to keep them
  up to date on what is happening.

— *Questionnaires and surveys*
  Questionnaires can be an effective method of collecting
  information from a large number of people about local

needs and help develop awareness of the project.
Responses will help develop your ideas about the re-use
of the building. Make sure your sample is scientifically
representative and statistically reliable.

— *Open days*
RTH has worked with groups that have held 'open days',
when local people were able to visit the building and talk
to members of the Partnership about its future. It provides
an opportunity for the Partnership to present its ideas, get
people involved and raise the project's profile. Inviting the
local press may be useful. You should set out your thoughts
on the future of the building and if your proposals receive a
poor reception from the majority of visitors it may be wise
to return to first principles and re-examine your objectives.

Possible activities for an 'open day' include guided
tours, study sessions to discuss illustrated proposals for
the building's re-use, and question and answer sessions.
Do remember to have some method by which people can
leave a note of their views, such as comment cards or a
visitors' book with room for people to make observations
and suggestions. Remember you may need public liability
insurance to run an open day.

Quayside Maltings, Mistley, Essex [case study]

The Quayside Maltings in the village of Mistley are Grade II Listed buildings that had been substantially vacant for 25 years. Many local people favoured demolition. However, others, recognising their historic link with the once-important local malting industry and the potential offered by a stunning location in the Georgian village centre overlooking the estuary of the River Stour, saw the potential for conservation and regeneration. With RTH help an Action Group (Partnership) of key local stakeholders was formed to consider options.

A range of ideas was discussed by the Action Group at a Planning Day when possibilities were matched against known local needs, opportunities and market conditions. A mixture of residential, work place, community and pub/café uses was agreed.

Local opinion was sceptical. Recognising that few people had actually been inside the building, the Action Group, with the co-operation of the owner and a developer, secured funding to refurbish a small part of the building, cleaning the brick work and ironwork, and renewing windows and doors to original patterns. The transformation was immediate. An 'Open Day' was held when the public could see inside and inspect an exhibition of the Action Group's proposals. Over 700 people visited and support for the proposals was almost unanimous.

This was followed by further Planning Days, widened to include many more interested organisations and individuals, to consider the proposals, by then subjected to a consultant's appraisal. A day-long event amended the vision to reflect market advice on costs, tilting the balance towards a more commercial approach whilst still maintaining the principal ambitions of the community. The new proposal was for 100,000 square feet of residential use and a restaurant/café and workshops led by the private sector, with a Community Trust developing the remainder of the Maltings for artists' studios, exhibition space, high quality workspace (to generate income and cross subsidise lower value areas) and community use (for performance/display/meeting space).

42

7

OWNERSHIP AND STATUTORY POWERS

If your building is in benevolent ownership and a re-use solution can be developed that does not conflict with the owner's interests, you will be able to make more rapid progress. If, however, the owner wishes to use your interest to maximise the resale value of their asset, as is more often the case, the following information can provide you with some ammunition.

If a building is Listed, owners have a duty of care towards its upkeep. However, if the cost of repairing or restoring a Listed building is greater than its resale value owners may have little incentive to invest in maintenance and repair. This can result in:

— Owners waiting for the condition of buildings to become so poor that they can make a case for demolition

— Owners requesting planning permission for a large amount of new development around the Listed building, claiming that profits from this are required to subsidise repair of the historic structures (often called 'enabling development')

— Owners seeking to redevelop the building in a way that destroys or damages its historic importance

Statutory powers

Do encourage your local authority to maintain pressure on the owner to fulfil their obligations. There are many statutory powers that can be used to do this.

1 Listing

Anyone can apply to have a historic building **Listed**. However, it must fulfil certain criteria in order to be Listed, so make sure your case is as strong as possible. Your local conservation or planning officer, or failing that **English Heritage, Cadw, Historic Scotland** or **Environment and Heritage Service** in Northern Ireland, can advise on the relevant points you need to make.

In England the Secretary of State has the power to **spot list** a building in imminent danger of demolition. This provides a breathing space for other options to be considered. Similar arrangements exist in Scotland, Wales and Northern Ireland.

2 Conservation Area

The Partnership's building may be unlisted but in a **Conservation Area**. There is a general presumption in favour of retaining unlisted historic buildings that make a positive contribution to the overall character or appearance of a Conservation Area.

Conservation Area Consent is required for the demolition of all, or substantially all, of an unlisted building in a Conservation Area. Unlisted buildings in Conservation Areas can also be eligible for certain **English Heritage** and **Heritage Lottery Fund** grants.

[see Chapter 1]

You will already know whether the Partnership's building is on a **Buildings at Risk** register: its inclusion may assist your case for grant aid, and encourage the local authority to take statutory steps. Statutory powers exist to prevent loss of, or damage to, historic buildings. If a historic building in your area is deteriorating you might wish to persuade your local authority to use its powers of intervention.

3 Building Preservation Notice

For unlisted buildings of architectural and historic interest in danger of demolition or significant alteration.

Local authorities can serve a **Building Preservation Notice** on the owner of any unlisted building of architectural and historic interest that is considered in danger of demolition or alteration that would detract from its cultural value. A Building Preservation Notice carries similar protection to listing but takes immediate effect and is usually faster than the spot listing procedure. This is essential in cases when a building is in imminent danger.

4 Urgent Works Notice

For any Listed building, or unlisted building which is important to the character of a Conservation Area.

If a historic building, or part of it, is in such poor condition that damage may become irreversible, local authorities have the power to serve an **Urgent Works Notice**. In Northern

Ireland **Environment and Heritage Service** has this power. This gives the owner a week in which to commence specified works. If work does not start within this time the serving agency has the power to enter the site, undertake the work and reclaim the costs from the owner.

An Urgent Works Notice can direct an owner to:

— Make a building weather-tight
— Enable a building to dry out
— Make a building safe from structural collapse
— Make a building secure to prevent illegal entry, vandalism and theft

The local authority can also apply to the Secretary of State for permission to serve an Urgent Works Notice on an unlisted building that is important to the character of a Conservation Area.

5 Repairs Notice

For any Listed building, but not for unlisted buildings in a Conservation Area.

Local authorities – or, in Northern Ireland, **Environment and Heritage Service** – can serve a **Repairs Notice** in respect of a Listed building at risk due to inadequate maintenance by the owner.

The kinds of work that can be specified in a Repairs Notice are more extensive than those of an Urgent Works Notice and include:

— Essential preliminary works to comply with health and safety regulations, e.g. decontamination, asbestos removal
— Comprehensive repairs to the structural envelope, roof structure, roof covering, chimney-stacks and flues, brick/ stone masonry or other construction materials, timber-frame, external finishes and cladding, rainwater goods and flashing
— Measures to secure general structural stability in accordance with specialist structural engineering advice
— Repair/reinstatement of external joinery, ironwork and architectural features
— Internal structural repairs to floors, ceilings, walls and partitions
— Repair and reinstatement of internal finishes – including plasterwork and floor surfaces

7

- Basic internal and external redecoration
- Repair/reinstatement of internal joinery, staircases, features and fittings
- Works to enable the building to be capable of beneficial use, such as repairs to, or reinstatement of, missing services
- Repairs to boundary walls, gates, railings, and associated fittings, surfaces, pathways and entrance steps
- Installation of additional security measures to prevent vandalism or unauthorised access following completion of works

6 Compulsory Purchase Order

The follow-up to a Repairs Notice, if the owner has failed to respond adequately.

If an owner fails to respond adequately to a Repairs Notice and the local authority can demonstrate to the Secretary of State that the owner has not taken reasonable steps to preserve the building or undertake necessary repairs, a **Compulsory Purchase Order** can be issued two months after a Repairs Notice has been served.

In most cases the threat of a Repairs Notice will prompt the owner either to carry out repairs or sell the building. The latter provides an opportunity for your Partnership to register its interest in acquiring it, either by negotiation from the owner, or from the local authority, should it proceed with a Compulsory Purchase Order. If the Partnership can secure the necessary funding, a 'back to back' agreement with the local authority may be possible. This usually means the local authority uses its powers to compulsorily purchase the building, before selling it to the Partnership or a trust established for the purpose of its conservation and development. The local authority is more likely to proceed with the compulsory purchase if it knows it has an enthusiastic new owner able to take on the building.

However, remember that your Partnership will need to have all its proposals agreed and be certain that it has the finance in place to assume such a responsibility.

8

UNDERSTANDING THE BUILDING AND DEFINING THE VISION

From the outset you need to know as much as possible about your building, including its history, architecture, structure, materials, condition, site and contents. You will also need to know if there are any ownership issues, statutory designations or published policies that might affect its future. Your ability to make changes to the building will be constrained by the planning system and legislation affecting the conservation and protection of heritage buildings and, of course, if you don't own it the owner will have a view.

[see Contacts]

This chapter gives guidance on methods of compiling information about your building and its conservation needs. The process of understanding your building runs parallel to the formation of your Partnership, discussed in earlier chapters. By following the processes outlined in this Handbook your Partnership will generate much of the information needed for a Conservation Management Plan. Every Plan will differ depending on the scale and needs of the building. The Heritage Lottery Fund has produced important guidance, available on its website. [www.hlf.org.uk]

Getting to know your building

It is important to take time to familiarise yourselves well with your building and its site. You will need a good up-to-date site plan and if one does not already exist you should produce or commission one. It is invaluable.

You can then structure your understanding by compiling a written Gazetteer or '**Room Book**' for the building. A Room Book is the descriptive counterpart to the Conservation Management Plan. It involves analysing and describing every component of every room of the building in a systematic manner, both for physical characteristics and condition. This does not require specialist knowledge, merely an observant eye. Photographs, plans and sketches can be used to support written descriptions.

Non-professionals do not always fully appreciate or notice all the features of their buildings and this exercise is a good way to get to grips with the detail – to understand the nature of each part and element. In this way you will be less likely to overlook important characteristics or inadvertently develop proposals that may cause damage. For example, the following questions might apply to a single room:

Floor:
— What is it made of?
— Is it constructed of the same material throughout or are there variations?
— If there are variations then show the pattern of different materials on a plan
— What is its condition?
— Do any parts look structurally unstable?
— Are parts obscured?
— Are you unsure of its material composition or structural integrity, or any parts of it? If so, describe which parts

Ask the same questions for walls, windows, doors, columns, beams and joists, ceiling, room fixtures and fittings.

Compiling a Room Book is not only a good way to understand the physical characteristics of the building but can also provide a useful foundation for a Conservation Statement or Conservation Management Plan and help reduce the associated costs and time.

Your proposals for the building should respect its architectural and historic importance, working with the 'grain' of its historic fabric. The building will have to change but your aim is to achieve 'appropriate change'. Your Partnership should not aim to preserve the building in aspic, but, instead, conserve its essential heritage elements and historic significance.

Conservation means all the processes of looking after a place so as to retain its cultural significance. It includes maintenance and may according to circumstances include preservation, restoration, reconstruction and adaptation and will commonly be a combination of more than one of these.

Any plan for the reuse of a historic building should, therefore, begin with an examination of its cultural significance, which should also reflect its significance to the community. This should be followed by an analysis of what needs to be done, or not done, if this cultural and community significance is to be retained. If a reuse proposal is developed without a proper comprehension of the place's cultural significance then an important dimension of the nation's cultural heritage could be lost forever.

Writing a Conservation Statement

A Conservation Management Plan is usually a detailed document which a specialist prepares. A **Conservation Statement** is a shorter and less detailed version which can sometimes be prepared by the Partnership on the basis of existing knowledge. However, it will not be comprehensive. While it may be unwise to develop major new proposals on the basis of a Statement alone, as it rarely includes enough information, it may be useful in the following circumstances:
— For small or straightforward heritage asset or where there are no major development proposals
— Before you prepare a brief for a full Conservation Management Plan
— As an exercise to think about issues in the early stages of developing a big project
— As a way of working out what gaps in knowledge exist early in the planning process
— To bring people together early in the process if it is to be prepared in-house

Your Statement should be logically structured to show that you have identified and assessed the buildings' cultural significance, and understand the opportunities and threats presented by proposals for its regeneration. It should show that you have developed proposals and policies for changes and adaptations that are appropriate and enable the building to be properly managed and maintained.

1 Description of the building and its condition
The Statement should begin with an inventory of each element of the building and site. The Statement should briefly describe the condition of each of the elements of the building you have

identified. If you have prepared a Room Book you will already have undertaken much of the work required for this section. You may wish to summarise your Room Book in the main text or include it as an appendix.

2 Understanding the building and its setting
The purpose of this section is to make the case for conserving and regenerating the building, drawing attention to all its important and historically valuable elements. Research the historical context of the building and the uses to which it was put, describe the phases of construction, beginning with the oldest, and any subsequent significant alterations.

3 Identification and assessment of significance
Identifying the cultural significance of a historic building can often be a specialised task, depending on its type and age. To the non-professional one collection of old rusting machines may look very similar to any other, but it may be that the objects under investigation could be highly significant, perhaps as the earliest or last surviving examples of a particular technological procedure and, therefore, must be conserved. For complex buildings, or those containing in situ machinery or artefacts, you may need a suitably experienced conservation architect or architectural historian to research its historical and architectural significance. Their conclusions can then be integrated with the descriptive inventory to show how the building's significance is dependent on the presence of historic structures and elements, and where there is a more general significance that relates to the whole site. It will also be possible to identify those parts of the building that do not contribute to, or may even detract from, its cultural significance and may be suited to modification or removal.

4 Overall proposals
You should include general details of the Partnership's intentions for the re-use of the building. This is so that a maintenance-philosophy can be devised that is realistic in relation to the intended uses and available resources, and any issues that could conflict with the significance of the site can be recognised and resolved early on.

5 Threats to significance

The purpose of this part of the Conservation Statement is to identify how the cultural significance of the building or site has been, is being, or could be compromised. When this is known, both for the building as a whole and for each of its significant parts, policies can then be developed to prevent an adverse impact. Summarise the issues and threats that may affect the building, which might include:

— Deteriorating condition
— Actions of the owners
— Inadequate statutory protection
— Environmental problems
— Inappropriate use, either in the past or proposed
— Lack of ongoing maintenance
— Pressure for development
— Political influence
— Vandalism, theft, fire, natural disaster

6 Protecting the building's significance – Conservation Policies

The early parts of the Statement will be largely analytical, assessing the various qualities of the whole of the building and each of its constituent parts. The Statement should conclude with a set of conservation policies to indicate how the building can be treated in its future use and maintenance. Rather than listing each action that might be taken to ensure the retention of the building's cultural significance, this section groups together similar issues into more general strategic conservation policies. Developing a set of strategic policies establishes a conservation-philosophy, or vision, for the building, and a framework and reference point for all future project development work.

Writing a Conservation Management Plan

A **Conservation Management Plan** is a document that helps you look after your historic building or site and addresses how any changes are to be planned. It explains why the building matters to people and sets out what should be done to look after it in any future use, alteration, development, change of use or repair by focussing on heritage rather than financial management. This is a detailed document that sets out the significance of the building or site as a heritage asset and identifies all the actions needed to conserve that significance, including management and maintenance. It should be based on a good understanding of the building and its condition, and is likely to involve consultation with different stakeholders.

Several key funders, such as the **Heritage Lottery Fund** and **English Heritage** (and their equivalents in other UK countries: **Cadw, Historic Scotland** and the **Environment and Heritage Service** in Northern Ireland) require a Conservation Management Plan to accompany major funding applications.

The first step in commissioning a Conservation Management Plan is to prepare a **Brief** to send to prospective consultants, setting out exactly what you would like them to do. Use the *conservation management plans checklists* and *conservation management plans model brief* produced by the **Heritage Lottery Fund** for guidance as a starting point. [www.hlf.org.uk] A plan that does not contain the information in the HLF checklist is unlikely to be of use to anyone managing a site or developing a project.

Conservation Management Plan contents should include:
— Stakeholders
— Understanding the asset
— History and context
— Social history
— Management information
— Field survey, gazetteer and inventory
— Typology (optional)
— Significance
— Issues and vulnerability
— Conservation management policies
— Maintenance plan
— Heritage impact assessment

Preparing the Brief will help you work out how detailed the plan should be and how much it might cost. It is a good idea for your Partnership to work on the Brief together, and consult major stakeholders, as this gives everyone ownership of the process.

The Vision Statement

By now the Partnership will have a fairly good idea of the range of uses that will command the widest support and potentially be the most viable, subject to detailed technical evaluation. You will also understand your building's cultural significance. You now have sufficient information to agree a **Vision Statement** for the building. A Vision Statement should describe your key aims. It will also help people to understand what the Partnership is trying to achieve, and the boundaries within which the project will develop. Effectively a 'branding' exercise it will also make the project easier to market to funding bodies, potential occupants and the community, all of whose support is needed.

The Partnership's Vision Statement should describe the key aims. These may be very broad but will define the single vision around which uses for the building will evolve. For example:

> We wish to conserve the historic and architectural character of the building so that it can continue to enrich our local environment, and provide resources and opportunities needed by the local community

Your Vision Statement could include some detailed aims such as:

— Developing the sustainable vitality and economic viability of the area
— Retaining the area's mixed-use character
— Retaining and re-using the building, so conserving the historic environment
— Creating jobs for local people by establishing work training schemes and workspace units
— Providing a variety of housing, especially for young people
— Reducing the need to commute from the area
— Enhancing the quality of the public realm
— Providing better community facilities
— Enabling controlled public access to the restored buildings

The Vision Statement and aims should express how your proposals for the building reflect its established historic character, are sustainable, and appropriate for the local community.

Conway Mill, Belfast [Case study]

Conway Mill is a flax spinning mill of a type that once dominated Belfast. Production ceased in 1975 and it suffered neglect and vandalism. In 1987, 49 such mills remained in the city but by 1998 this had reduced to 20, of which Conway was the only one with the full range of principal site components. It was Listed (Grade B2) in1999.

In 1982 a community group, Conway Street Community Enterprises, acquired the Mill for social and economic regeneration, initially using the largely unrestored buildings for new purposes, and only raising money for maintenance. However, it recognised that it owned an asset of historic significance and resolved to restore it in a way that conserved its importance to the community and took account of its architectural qualities.

With RTH advice the Group agreed to produce a Conservation Plan to set out the characteristics and significance of the Mill, and how it might be adapted and conserved. Group members also undertook a survey of local people to record their memories of the building and the work that took place in it. They held an exhibition of photographs and documents that attracted more people, who in turn provided further information about 'life in the mill'. The Group commissioned research into the social and economic conditions in

Belfast at the time of the construction of the Mill, which helped them understand its former role in the life of the city.

The Group then researched the internal organisation of the Mill, including the many trades and job types, and undertook a detailed room-by-room survey to identify and record features, such as foot-baths, stone flag floors, iron columns, brick arched ceilings, ceramic tiles, roof and fenestration detailing, boilers and machinery, architectural detailing, and the various phases of construction. This gave Group members a detailed grasp of the characteristics of the Mill and how it had worked in industrial uses. This enabled them to write a clear brief for the preparation of a Conservation Plan.

They required the Plan to set out their vision for the restored building; the extent to which changes would, and would not, be acceptable; the role of any new build and new materials; and arrangements for visitor access By researching the characteristics of the Mill, and its important social role and function, the Group came to know their building. This helped them ensure that the Conservation Plan produced clear guidance for the subsequent development and restoration proposals.

9

FEASIBILITY STUDY

Writing a Vision Statement is good preparation for the next stage, which is preparing a Brief for consultants undertaking your Feasibility Study.

All major funding bodies now require a **Feasibility Study** with their applications. A Feasibility Study should do the following:
— Set out the purposes for which funding is sought
— Contain an Options Appraisal of a range of proposed new uses
— Fit the proposed new uses to the building and its location, or demonstrate what is or is not appropriate
— Show how the Partnership's objectives can be met
— Demonstrate that the project is viable
— Provide a tool that can be used to promote the project to potential supporters and decision-makers
— Form the basis of the Partnership's subsequent business plan, design proposals and funding application

A Feasibility Study is designed to subject your proposals to external professional assessment and financial scrutiny. It tests whether, and how, these proposals can be structured to ensure success, and undertakes an Options Appraisal of different mixes of preferred uses. It highlights the financial implications of essential construction and refurbishment work, tests alternative capital funding options, and evaluates revenue flow assumptions. The purpose is to establish that the proposed project is appropriate, realistic and economically sustainable.

The Feasibility Study must be carried out objectively and professionally, with the assistance of independent consultants. Producing a Feasibility Study is a costly and time-consuming activity, so must be backed by a well-formulated **Brief** from your Partnership.

Feasibility Study Brief

The Brief sets out your knowledge of the constraints and opportunities the building and area offer, and your objectives and expectations – as already developed during your meetings and public consultation. The Brief is not meant to preclude new ways of meeting your objectives; rather, it should be a guide for the consultants. Any other documents produced in developing your project proposals should support and accompany the Feasibility Study Brief.

As your building is of historic importance it is fundamental that your Feasibility Study includes an evaluation of its physical and historic characteristics, normally in the form of a [see Chapter 8] **Conservation Statement** or a **Conservation Management Plan**. This is best undertaken by an architect, archaeologist or surveyor with experience of heritage conservation, depending on the size and complexity of your building.

You will need to consolidate your understanding of the building's historical and architectural attributes by commissioning a **structural survey** by a qualified surveyor or architect with experience of historic buildings. This will allow you to understand the physical strengths and weaknesses of the building and make an initial assessment of its ability to accommodate change. It should also set out proposals and costings for repair, which should include justification for works on the structure, and the arrangements to be set in place to ensure its continued maintenance afterwards. You can contract this work as part of the main feasibility study, or as separate pieces of work.

There are several ways to structure your Brief, so the following is only a suggestion. Remember to address the requirements of each section and provide any information that will help your consultants. Although it is an obvious point, any research work the Partnership has undertaken to date may be wasted unless your consultants know about it.

Be as specific as you can, otherwise your consultants may undertake work you do not require but for which you will still have to pay.

The following pages contain a proforma **Feasibility Study Brief** based on the combined experience of the Architectural Heritage Fund and RTH. Try to keep your Brief short (10 –15 pages) so that the consultants know exactly what you want.

1 Background

Aim to provide your consultants with the following information:

— The building's location, description, current status and condition

— The building's historic and architectural importance, so that any options proposed are consistent with your requirement to retain its significance

— The statutory designations relating to the area or building, e.g. located in a Conservation Area, Listed building etc

— The building's development potential and current ownership status. Any structural surveys and reports should be attached as appendices and reference made to them in the main text

— The background to your Partnership and how it developed its interest in the building; the Partnership's overall aims and objectives, achievements, membership, skills and abilities

— Why the building is at risk e.g. redundancy, physical vulnerability/awkwardness, planning restrictions, access, owner's attitude, local property market

— The planning context e.g. uses defined in the Local Plan

— Your understanding of the area in which the building is located e.g. any social or economic information produced by local authorities or other economic regeneration agencies

— The relationship between the project and any other initiatives planned or already operational in the area

— How your ideas have been developed. Include relevant reports as appendices or direct the consultants to where they can be obtained

— How you see the building being re-used and how each use will contribute to your objectives. You should include your Vision Statement as an appendix.

2 Scope of the Feasibility Study

Define the specific issues you require your consultants to report upon so that the development of the study is controlled within definite boundaries. For example, you may wish your consultants to:

— Report on the cost of repairing the building in accordance with your requirements. By understanding what should, or should not, be done with the building, your consultants will find it easier to identify a balance of uses that are compatible with its character.

— Illustrate their outline proposals, taking into account:
  - Existing potential demand
  - Appropriateness of use within the building and location
  - Impact upon the building, the area and existing businesses
  - Space and servicing requirements
  - Future management
  - Sources of potential funding
  - A viable development programme
  - A financial analysis
  - Project costs, including management costs, fees, finance costs, insurance, VAT etc
  - Deficit to be bridged (the 'heritage deficit')
  - Working capital requirement, including cost, security and timing
  - Appraisal of capital and revenue costs, including long-term financing and management costs
  - Cash flow projections: for the development phase and following three years
  - Valuations: current and following repair
  - Resale and/or other income from the building once repaired for re-use

Make sure your consultants are aware that they must provide clear conclusions, recommendations and implementation strategies.

3 Strategic context and the objectives of the project
List the aims your Partnership has developed with reference to your Vision Statement. Your consultants will need to demonstrate that your values and objectives are reflected in the final proposals. They also need to show the philosophy they have used to approach the project, and how the building's importance will be protected and enhanced.

4 Assessment of need / commercial demand
Set out any information about the monetary and non-monetary issues you have identified and indicate where you want your consultants to undertake further work. For example, you may want them to look at rent levels for commercial floor-space.

5 Possible new uses

Set out your suggestions for new uses in the building but make it clear that this is not intended to constrain consideration of other proposals. If there are some uses that must be represented for your Partnership's objectives to be met, make sure to state them here. Similarly, explain any specific requirements about how you want the building to be re-used, e.g. the maximum amount of space to be taken up by any one use or tenant. The consultant should fully explain their preferred scheme and the benefits that will derive from this.

6 Other considerations

You may want to set your consultants specific tasks such as:
— Tackling access and parking arrangements
— Proposing a marketing strategy for the project

7 Programme and process

Provide timescales and deadlines for the production of the various phases of the work. You can obtain guidance on this from RTH, the **Architectural Heritage Fund**, the **Association of Preservation Trusts** or, sometimes, your local authority. Set out arrangements for administering the tendering process, including which groups and individuals will be evaluating the tenders received.

8 Contact information

Include names and contact details of people who have helped you develop your proposal: your consultants may want to talk to them.

9 Appendices

Provide any background research or technical information [see Chapter 11] that may be helpful. This will save time for the consultant and money for you.

While the Brief is being written other members of the Partnership should be working to procure funds to pay for the Feasibility Study and any other ongoing costs.

Birnbeck Pier, Weston-super-Mare, Somerset [case study]

Birnbeck Pier is a Grade II* Listed pleasure pier linking Weston-super-Mare to Birnbeck Island. It was designed by Eugenius Birch and built in 1867, becoming popular for its fairground attractions and as a steamer arrival point from Wales. The construction of the Severn Bridge and increasing popularity of foreign holidays led to a decline in visitors and the last scheduled sailing was in 1979. The Pier closed in 1994, although the RNLI continue to operate a lifeboat station from the Island. It is considered one of the five most important British piers and was placed on the Buildings at Risk Register in 2002.

RTH and North Somerset Council created a Partnership of stakeholders to develop proposals to save the Pier from dereliction and bring it back into use. A Planning Day considered options and agreed that the Pier and Island should be conserved both for their historic and architectural value, and as a catalyst for wider regeneration in the town. The Partnership formed itself into a Trust and agreed to appoint consultants to report on the structural condition of the Pier and associated buildings, provide costings for repair and new build, and test proposals for sustainable new uses that would generate the visitor flow and income needed to operate and maintain the structures. It agreed a Brief for a Feasibility Study that reflected its aspirations.

Key Project Objectives were to rescue a national landmark, conserve the historic structure, promote appropriate and sustainable uses, promote public access and create jobs.

From these and other objectives the Trust generated possible re-uses for evaluation, including: RNLI, food and drink, hotel, steamers, and all year round high-value businesses.

Other possible uses were suggested, such as conference, education and interpretation facilities, boating, and a wedding venue. Some ideas were also ruled out, such as traditional seaside amusements, and intensive residential or marina uses. Considerations about how the Pier should relate to the town were set out, as were possible links to steamer routes in the Bristol Channel. This Feasibility Study Brief gave the consultants a framework of client expectations. Work was packaged in two tenders: team one to undertake the structural engineering, architectural conservation, marine ecology, quantity surveying and design work; team two to undertake the valuation, economic appraisal and niche marketing work.

Key tasks were specified for each team, together with the professional expertise required. Consultants were asked to provide three or four realistic and sustainable economic options, and costings for all the work. The Trust was able to score tenders against the Brief using pre-agreed criteria, and select the winning teams. The final costs were approximately £50,000. The Trust could then use the Feasibility Study report to develop its preferred option further.

10

APPOINTING AND MANAGING CONSULTANTS

Your Partnership will need to appoint a reputable consultancy that possesses (or can call upon) the necessary range of expertise to do the work set out in the Feasibility Study Brief. The 'lead' professional should be a conservation architect or engineer, a conservation-trained building surveyor, a town planner with conservation experience, or, depending on the project, possibly an economist with business planning skills. Whatever their discipline they must have a track record with similar historic buildings. The lead professional can then bring in the services of experts from other disciplines where their input is required.

Inviting consultants to tender

Firms should have good general experience of conservation, and be comfortable with schemes of the size proposed. Those offering highly specialised services (e.g. historically accurate restoration of buildings) should probably be avoided.

Suggestions or advice on suitable companies can be sought from your local authority's planning department or conservation team; the regional office of **English Heritage, Cadw**, the **Environment and Heritage Service** in Northen Ireland or **Historic Scotland**; the **Architectural Heritage Fund**; a local building preservation trust; or a community organisation that has commissioned similar studies.

Most funding bodies will require you to have obtained quotations from at least two lead consultants, but it is advisable to invite three or four. Be aware of the costs to consultants involved in tendering and only invite those you would be willing to appoint.

Ask consultants to submit a proposal detailing:
— An outline of the scope of each section of the study
— A method statement
— Professional details and recent experience of the people who will do the work
— Proposed timetable for undertaking the work
— How much time each member of the team will contribute
— Fee for the study
— Confirmation of professional indemnity cover to a level appropriate to the project

Use this as a guide when short-listing – it shows whether the consultants have understood your brief and its expected results, and indicate their level of experience, enthusiasm and how they propose to undertake the work.

Drawing up a short-list
If the appropriate range of firms has been invited to submit tenders, those received should be broadly similar. The procedure for short-listing should be formal, with applicants scored against agreed criteria. You should set these out on a scoring sheet before you start. A systematic approach can reveal detailed insights that may not otherwise be apparent – remember the slickest, or cheapest, submission is not necessarily the best. Bear in mind that unsuccessful consultants might ask for feedback and so you will need to explain and justify your decision.

Interviewing consultants
The interview panel should consist of members of your Partnership and external advisers on architecture, regeneration and conservation. You could invite officers from the local authority's planning and economic development departments, or an organisation with experience of conservation projects, to join your panel as advisers.

The interview provides an opportunity to assess the overall experience of each consultant and their approach to historic buildings. Each should be afforded equal time to explain their bids, and be heard without interruption.

The interview should address the following issues:
— *Staffing*: the skills and experience of those staff actually undertaking the work, and the relevance of their CVs
— *Understanding the Brief*: the reasons for the project and the outcomes expected from the feasibility study

— *Conservation issues*: understanding of the conservation and architectural considerations
— *Previous experience*: good previous experience of restoring and adapting historic buildings is vital
— *Community participation*: experience of community-led projects
— *Market research*: further research which the consultant believes is needed
— *Financial analysis*: how the financial forecast will be assessed
— *Funding*: experience of funding applications and dealing with relevant funding bodies

Making the decision

Your Partnership must feel confident that it can establish a good working relationship with the successful consultants. Also, bear in mind these key matters:
— Quality of the written submission
— Performance at the interview
— The consultant's experience of relevant conservation projects

During the study

Your Partnership should keep in close contact with the consultants during the study. Make sure that you receive interim written reports on progress, and that discussions include an opportunity for the Partnership to give its own feedback. In the absence of a focused report on the issues you will end up making generalist observations of little value. Close involvement will maintain control of the study's direction and ensure that the consultants are responding to and developing the Partnership's ideas, not simply developing their own!

As work progresses you must pay 'stage payments', a proportion of the consultancy fees agreed at the time of the appointment. The initial findings should be presented to the Partnership in draft form for feedback before the final report is prepared. You should set aside sufficient time to consider the draft, give feedback, question the consultants on the logic, reasoning and nature of their proposals, and give instructions on any necessary amendments for the final report. Make sure the report meets any criteria laid down by bodies funding the feasibility study.

Harvey's Foundry, Hayle, Cornwall [case study]

Harvey's Foundry in Hayle, Cornwall, once produced steam pumping engines, initially for Cornwall's deep tin and copper mines and then for export across the world. At one time 80 per cent of the world's steam pumping engines were produced in Hayle.

By the 1970s much of Harvey's Foundry and the adjacent harbour were demolished and there was widespread public concern at the loss of the town's heritage. The Harvey's Foundry Regeneration Group and then Hayle Town Trust developed proposals to conserve and regenerate what remained, and in 1998 RTH, with support from Penwith District Council, established a Partnership representing the key stakeholder interests. This subsequently established the Harvey's Foundry Trust as the vehicle to implement regeneration proposals.

The Partnership recognised that quality restoration would take time, funding regimes were geared to projects that generate jobs, and public expectation was for instant results.

The solution was an imaginative balance between these considerations. Phase I would commence in the Grade II* Listed former Foundry Drawing Office, which fronted the town square. There was to be a modern 8,000 square-feet building on a vacant part of the site for new businesses as a sign that new jobs were being created and the best way to attract grant aid. The new building was designed in sympathy with the adjacent

historic Foundry buildings. Phase 1 would be a quick win and generate an income from tenants to fund the Trust.

The Partnership directed the detailed technical evaluations, conservation studies, options appraisal and business planning studies. Its clarity of vision gathered support from funders, including English Heritage and Penwith District Council who grant-aided and acquired part of the site. The Partnership assembled a funding cocktail of £1.98 million funding for Phase I: Penwith Council (£242,000), Hayle Town Council (£1,000), English Heritage (£60,000), Heritage Economic Regeneration Scheme (£287,000), South West of England RDA (£150,000), Single Regeneration Budget (£242,000), Cornwall County Council (£60,000), Cornwall Enterprise (£140,000), European Union Objective One Programme (£797,000).

The project is now central to the regeneration of Hayle. It has demonstrated that conserving and then using industrial heritage can create new jobs and opportunities. The project's high profile enabled the local authority to attract further funds for other heritage buildings in the town.

The Partnership subsequently secured funds from the Townscape Heritage Initiative (funded by the Heritage Lottery Fund) for Phase II to conserve and adapt more of the remaining Foundry buildings. Phase III is in the pipeline. Nothing succeeds like success!

11

FUNDING SOURCES

Consultants will examine sources of funding for the main project but the Partnership must raise funds to meet the costs of drawing up the Brief, organising consultation days, marketing the project's aims, and so on. Your Partnership will have been cultivating potential funding partners already but the following is a brief guide to generic funding sources. Contacts for all the organisations mentioned are included in the Contacts section at the end of this Handbook.

General geographical sources of funding

England and Wales

The **Architectural Heritage Fund** (AHF) publishes annually *Funds for Historic Buildings in England and Wales – A Directory of Sources.* This lists funding sources for those repairing, conserving and converting historic buildings, including statutory and other public sources for special projects (e.g. non-secular buildings) and relevant charitable trusts. It also lists other funding sources whose main remit lies elsewhere (e.g. regeneration or housing) but which may support historic [see Contacts] building projects that contribute to its own objectives.

Scotland

The **Scottish Civic Trust** publishes *Sources of Financial Help for Scotland's Historic Buildings.* Some of the sources in the AHF's *Funds for Historic Buildings in England and Wales* [see above] also [see Contacts] apply in Scotland.

Northern Ireland

The **Ulster Architectural Heritage Society** (UAHS) publishes a *Directory of Funds for Historic Buildings in Northern Ireland.* Some of the sources in the AHF's *Funds for Historic Buildings in [see Contacts] England and Wales* [see above] also apply in Northern Ireland.

Statutory funding

National heritage agencies

English Heritage; Cadw (Welsh Historic Monuments); Historic Scotland; and Environment and Heritage Service in Northern Ireland have different programmes and their budgets vary from year to year. They may be able to provide some grant assistance depending on how historically important they deem your building to be, but it is not likely to be a large sum. However, it is really helpful to have some funding – even a small amount – from these sources, as this strengthens your credibility with other funders.

[see Contacts]

Europe

The European Regional Development Fund (ERDF) provides support for projects contributing to the development of regions identified as economically in need and that meet the Fund's objectives. Eligible schemes include built heritage projects contributing to the economic development of an area through, for example, providing local employment or boosting tourism. Only a very small area of the UK is eligible for ERDF support under its Objective One and Objective Two programmes. For advice and application forms contact your regional Government Office.

Landfill Tax Credit Scheme

Landfill operators may claim a credit of up to 20 per cent against their landfill tax liability if they make a contribution to an approved environmental body. The scheme is regulated by ENTRUST [www.entrust.org.uk], a not-for-profit company approved by HM Customs and Excise. ENTRUST enrols qualifying organisations and ensures compliance with the scheme's regulations. In order to qualify, an organisation's objectives must meet one of those on the Customs and Excise list, which include 'the maintenance, repair and restoration of a building which is of historic or architectural interest'. The building must be accessible to the public and within ten miles of an active, licensed landfill site.

Local Authority Grants

Local Authorities can provide grants or loans for repair and maintenance of historic buildings. These are restricted to a maximum of 50 per cent of the estimated cost but in practice the percentage of costs that can be funded is usually much less. Some local authorities award grants for initial options appraisals. For more information contact the conservation officer or planning department in your local authority.

Regional development bodies

Regional Development Agencies (RDAs) promote sustainable economic development, and social and physical regeneration. They have substantial capital budgets and are responsible for administering the Single Regeneration Budget (SRB) (see below) for regeneration strategies and other related priorities. RDAs and local enterprise agencies are a good source of potential funding and may contribute to the cost of preparing a business plan. For more information contact your regional RDA [see Chapter 4] in England. Scotland, Wales and Northern Ireland have separate arrangements.

Special government regeneration initiatives
Your part of the country may be included in a targeted regeneration initiative funded by the Government e.g. a 'housing pathfinder' or neighbourhood renewal initiative. A single such programme may not cover every part of a local authority area. Contact the Office of the Deputy Prime Minister [www.odpm. gov.uk] to see if your project qualifies for aid under Single Regeneration Budget objectives in England. The devolved Parliament in Scotland and Assemblies in Wales and Northern Ireland have similar schemes.

Non-Government funding

The Architectural Heritage Fund (AHF)
The AHF is an independent national charity whose grant programme assists Building Preservation Trusts (BPTs) and other charities to meet the cost of appraising a historic building with [see Contacts] a view to re-using it. The AHF also provides low interest loans to help charities acquire, repair and conserve historic buildings.
— **Options Appraisal grants** (formerly Feasibility Study grants). The AHF offers grants of up to 75 per cent of the cost of a feasibility study, up to a maximum of £5,000 (£7,500 for exceptionally large or complex projects).
— **Refundable Project Development grants**, normally of a maximum of £15,000 covering specific professional fees and other post-feasibility study cost.

Arts Councils

Arts Councils in England, Wales, Scotland and Northern Ireland distribute Lottery funds for projects supporting the arts, including grants for feasibility studies and capital projects. Projects must have a minimum grant requirement of £5,000. For projects budgeted at less than £100,000 applicants must provide at least 10 per cent of the funding themselves; for projects costing more than £100,000, 25 per cent must come from the applicant. Projects must contain an arts-related component, such as a gallery, to be eligible. For more information contact your local **Arts Council**.

Heritage Lottery Fund (HLF)

The HLF provides grants for projects involving historic buildings of local, regional and national importance. HLF have regional offices which are a useful first point of contact. Full guidance and application forms are available from the HLF website [www.hlf.org.uk]. The HLF operates several funding programmes, the most relevant of which are:

— **Heritage grant** (£50,000 plus)

This programme offers grants of £50,000 or more to projects that conserve and enhance our diverse heritage, or encourage more people to be involved in their heritage, or both. Projects should also make sure that everyone can learn about, have access to and enjoy their heritage. Projects can include nature conservation, historic buildings, museum collections, archive collections, spoken history records, cultural traditions, and objects and sites relating to the UK's industrial, transport and maritime history.

These Heritage grants are available to not-for-profit organisations. The HLF will consider projects involving private owners as part of a joint application for educational and access schemes only. If private owners are involved you will need to show that the public benefit is greater than any private gain.

All projects must be led by a not-for-profit organisation.

— **Project Planning grant** (£5,000 to £50,000)

These grants are intended to support the cost of specialist reports that may be necessary to 'work up' your project, which you expect to lead to a full Heritage grant application.

These include:
— an access plan which involves research designed to improve access to the heritage;
— a conservation management plan to bring about a better understanding of a heritage site, collection or large object, and to set out how it will be managed to conserve its significance;
— an audience development plan which involves research to develop new audiences for the heritage;
— other types of necessary specialist conservation report, such as a structural survey or conservator's report.
— non-public-sector organisations can also apply for a Project Planning grant to support the cost of employing a suitably qualified and experienced person to help them plan their project.

Sports Lottery Fund

Scotland, England, Wales and Northern Ireland all have bodies that distribute lottery funds to upgrade buildings reserved entirely for sports use. If your project envisages several uses, these bodies will only offer funds for the sports component.
[www.lotterygoodcauses.org.uk]

Charitable and private sector funding

Unless your Trust already has private funds you should seek private and charitable help as well as public money. Private sector funders will provide a secondary tier of funding, but many require evidence of public funding.

Nowadays, obtaining funds from private sector sources calls for more than a clutch of begging letters. For some large projects a professional fundraiser may be needed. For any group considering this, remember:
— Understand the nature of private sector fundraising – its components, pre-requisites and culture
— Be aware of the need for a compelling, value-driven case that demonstrates the project's 'unique selling points'. Who delivers your message can also be as important as the message itself: call on patrons or people of status capable of being impressive and convincing. They will establish your credibility.

Private sector funders tend to prefer to donate to people, rather than buildings, so the Partnership must be ready to sell its ideas in a people-focused way:

— Ensure your project is capable of inspiring people, effectively as an expression of their own dreams and aspirations
— Engage people at every level, prompted by your enthusiasm and goals
— Forge long-term relationships. Your core values and aspirations must hold people's interest in order to ensure their continued commitment in the future

The private sector must be persuaded of the difference their funding will make. Giving is part of a two-way exchange in which donors feel they have made a worthwhile – and visible – contribution to the community. Goodwill and trust must be cultivated in order not to undermine future private sector support. Donors deserve to be treated with integrity and generosity.

Who gives?

Individuals
Generally, the public is generous in making charitable donations. You can raise money by means of a general appeal, but you may have more success if you can offer interested people a reciprocal experience, such as a social event, sponsored walk, open day or 'Buy a Brick' appeal.

Companies
Large multinationals generally do not have a particular interest in, or allegiance to, specific locations or communities. Sponsorship efforts should, therefore, be concentrated on local or regional firms (or national firms with regional offices) that might benefit from further positive local publicity. Build relationships with individuals who have a personal interest in furthering activities that could work in your building.

Trusts and charities
These are set up by companies, families or individuals to disburse funds for specific or general purposes. See *A Guide to the Major Trusts* published by The Directory of Social Change [www.dsc.org.uk].

Pre-requisites for successful major capital fundraising

You must tackle fund-raising in a professional and focussed way. Before making any approaches to potential funders check that your case can demonstrate you have:

— *Compelling case for support* that expresses the Partnership's vision, values and socio-economic arguments for sponsorship. You should have a realistic and achievable fundraising target coupled with a realistic business plan. Remember to 'customise' benefits to match donors' perceived or stated motivations

— *Identified sources of funds*
  These can be divided into three main categories:
  • Charitable Trusts that support regeneration projects
  • Individual benefactors
  • Corporate donors/ sponsors
  There will be potential for community fundraising after most (say 75 per cent) of the required capital is in place

— *Leadership* by committed, active people of influence in the community

— *The right resources*, management and organisational structure to research meticulously and prepare funding applications, or, if necessary, to employ a professional to draw up and implement fundraising plans

— *Key stages* and *timescale*

Although funds may be raised for a one-off project it makes sense, once you've attracted donors, to continue cultivating the help of those who would support beneficial work in your community.

Salt Warehouse and Number 4 Warehouse, Sowerby Bridge [case study]

The Wharf at Sowerby Bridge grew in the 18th and early 19th centuries as a trans-shipment point at the junction of the Rochdale Canal and the Calder and Hebble Navigation. With the closure of the Rochdale Canal its many Listed stone buildings fell into disuse or under-use. A combination of efforts by Sea Scouts, who used a Warehouse for their boats, and local business people, who recognised the potential, brought some buildings back into use. However, it was recognised that a strategy was needed for the Wharf which would fund a future for the largely vacant Salt and Number 4 Warehouses.

RTH created a Partnership to tackle this task which embraced the key stakeholders and the freeholder, British Waterways. It wanted to avoid gentrification and agreed a strategy based on retaining existing businesses; focusing on water-based recreation, such as canal boating; and attracting new high value businesses to offer jobs in skill-growth sectors. The Regional Development Agency, Yorkshire Forward, endorsed this approach and funded a new access road to the Wharf to sustain additional traffic, together with new lighting and parking. The road was built in traditional stone setts and the lighting was in keeping with the local character, establishing a standard for quality design. This was the first sign that something was happening.

Following several Planning Days to consider new uses for the Warehouses it was agreed that the Grade II Listed Salt be developed for offices, restaurant and interpretation centre, and the Number 4 for boat building (it had a wet dock in use) with workshops or offices on the upper floors. The Partnership also marketed the Wharf as a visitor destination, and public fundraising paid for a bronze sculpture at the Wharf entrance as an icon for the site.

While funding was secured from the Heritage Lottery Fund and British Waterways to refurbish the Warehouses, private sector investors regenerated other heritage buildings for restaurants, offices and retail uses. An unsightly scrap yard closed and the land developed for new-build apartments. Millions of pounds have been invested by the private sector, demonstrating the catalytic effect the regeneration of the Warehouses have had on the entire Wharf.

The result is a working community in a place of great beauty. The Warehouses have been conserved and regenerated in a way that largely retains their character while incorporating modern design, particularly in the form of a new external lift to the Number 4 Warehouse. As a result they won the 2005 Waterways Trust and British Urban Regeneration Association (BURA) Historic Environment Award [www.bura.org.uk].

12

PROJECT DELIVERY
AND THE FUTURE

As the Partnership is seeking, and will be handling, large amounts of money, it must now acquire an appropriate legal organisational structure. Most Partnerships will wish to acquire Charitable Trust and limited liability company status. Apart from the essential legal protection this provides, some funding bodies will usually only award grants to legally constituted charities.

Charitable status

— Organisations based in England or Wales can register as a charity if they meet the criteria of the Charity Commissioners
— Organisations based in Northern Ireland and Scotland must obtain confirmation of charitable status from the Inland Revenue
— *Starting a Charity and Applying for Registration*, An information pack about gaining charitable status, is available from The Charity Commission
   [www.charity-commission.gov.uk]

Securing charitable status confers a number of important advantages including:
— Access to grants from trusts, and certain statutory and public funding bodies
— Tax relief
— Reduced business rates for premises

You also need to consider registering for VAT exemption as this affects VAT treatment e.g. relief on capital building works. However, charitable status imposes restrictions on the type of work an organisation can undertake and the ways it can operate. The Charity Commission recognises the promotion of urban and rural regeneration for public benefit in areas of social and economic deprivation as a charitable purpose.

This can be achieved by the maintenance or improvement of the physical, social and economic infrastructure, and by assisting people who are disdvantaged by their social and economic circumstances. If you are unsure if your proposals and activities qualify, look at 'RR2 Promotion of Urban and Rural Regeneration' for tests for charitable status, available on the Charity Commission website [www.charity-commission.gov.uk].

An organisation cannot secure charitable status if it promotes a political agenda or a particular point of view as a primary objective. In order to be eligible for charitable status all the organisation's objectives must be charitable and all its activities must directly further those charitable objectives and be for public benefit. To establish a charitable organisation your objectives must, therefore, be clear and concise: they are difficult to change once charitable status has been secured. Charity law is currently under review and proposed new legislation is likely to widen the list of charitable objectives, including regeneration. Consult the Charity Commission website for the latest guidance.

Many projects, especially those with relatively uncomplicated re-use approved proposals, can be implemented using a Charity Commission approved model **Building Preservation Trust (BPT)** constitution.

Building Preservation Trusts are charities established to preserve buildings of architectural or historic interest, usually those where an economically viable solution is beyond the reach of both the original owner and the normal operation of the current market. Most BPTs are constituted as companies limited by guarantee with charitable status.

BPTs can be **Revolving Funds** or Trusts set up for a Single Project. A Revolving Fund BPT builds up a reserve of capital to use in its first project which when repaired and sold on can help to fund its next project. A Single Project BPT is set up for a single building, [see Contacts] which will be owned and maintained in perpetuity.

Most BPTs are members of the Association of Preservation Trusts (APT). The APT has a special relationship with the Architectural Heritage Fund (AHF), which can grant-aid feasibility study costs and provide low interest loans. For more information contact the AHF, who can supply model Memorandum and Articles of Association constitutions that have been approved by the Charity Commissioners. Arrangements in Scotland and Northern Ireland are different, and the AHF has also produced separate guidance notes for each.

Development Trusts

Development Trusts (sometimes known as Amenity Trusts) differ from BPTs in that they concentrate primarily on commercial activities involving people and places, as well as specific buildings. They are usually companies limited by guarantee with charitable status and some degree of community management. Such Trusts provide an effective way [see Contacts] of involving the community in improving its quality of life.

Project responsibility

It is a legal requirement for an organisation with charitable status to have a clearly identifiable Governing Body. Many Trusts are both a limited liability company and a charity. They have a Board of Non-Executive Directors (or Trustees) who are responsible for policy but not day-to-day management, which is usually delegated to employees.

Trustees have overall legal responsibility for the control and management of the organisation, with defined powers and responsibilities under both company law and charity law.

Individuals selected as Trustees should be chosen on the basis of relevant experience, their likely contribution and their willingness to play an active role. They should not be appointed because of their status or position in the community (this role is better fulfilled by honorary Presidents, Vice Presidents or Patrons). Bear in mind that some people involved in the Partnership up to this stage may not want to take on the formal, legal responsibility of being a Trustee. However, you can still involve these people as advisers on sub-committees or working parties, or by maintaining a general membership of supporters.

If a Trustee is in a position to provide professional services to the organisation their interest must be declared, and rigorous procedures observed before paid work is commissioned. Trustees are not entitled to payment for their duties apart from expenses.

You may wish to make specific provision for key bodies (such as the local authority) to have the right to nominate a Trustee. This will ensure a spread of accountable stakeholders, and will also help to tie in support for your venture.

12

The following roles must be fulfilled:

— *Chair* : conducts meetings, ensures action points are followed up and the governing document adhered to.

— *Company Secretary* : takes meeting minutes and is responsible for correspondence. A company limited by guarantee must appoint a Company Secretary, who is responsible for keeping proper accounts, which must be professionally audited and filed annually with Companies House. Returns must also be submitted annually to the Charity Commission. A Trustee can fill this post if it carries no salary or fee.

— *Treasurer* : responsible for the organisation's finances

Sub-committees

Depending on the size and complexity of your project, you may need to set up sub-committees or working groups separate from the Governing Body to undertake specific tasks. These must include some Trustees but can also include other interested parties and are a good way to bring in outside expertise for certain tasks. Trustees need to consider carefully those powers they wish to delegate as they will remain legally accountable for all actions.

Trading activities

Charities have a limited right to conduct trading activities provided these are connected to delivering their charitable objectives. Bear in mind that if the total amount earned by these activities amounts to more than £50,000 per year, you may be required to establish a separate trading company that can then gift its profits to your charity.

Project management

It will not be long before the amount of work to be done exceeds the capacity of your Partnership volunteers to do it and you will need some dedicated (usually part-time at first) assistance. You should put together a case for funding this work and present it to the regeneration agencies and your local authority. The AHF and the HLF may also consider making small grants for a projects officer. High quality project management skills are essential to ensure satisfactory completion of your project. Without them much of the preceding good work could be placed at risk.

[see Chapter 11]

The future

Having formed your Partnership into a charitable trust, embarked on raising funds, undertaken comprehensive local consultation, and completed a Feasibility Study and Conservation Management Plan, your Trust has made fantastic progress. You now understand the building you aim to bring back to life and the needs of the local community who will use it. Furthermore, the Trust is in the most positive position possible to raise funds to complete the conservation and redevelopment. Your Trust's job is now to ensure everyone involved remains enthusiastically committed to driving forward the project. A local building preservation trust may be willing to share its experience with your Trust at this point.

You will need to complete your fundraising and seek relevant permissions from the local planning authority, which will involve using a conservation architect to prepare plans and submit planning and listed building consent applications. The Trust should be as thorough as it was in appointing consultants for the Feasibility Study and Conservation Management Plan. In due course you will need to appoint a building contractor with experience of historic buildings. It might be also necessary to appoint a project manager to oversee the contract unless the project architect has been commissioned to do this.

Remember to keep the community informed about progress, and make sure everyone involved in the project is invited to celebrate the successful conclusion of each stage. Good luck!

CONTACTS

For a comprehensive directory of organisations, associations, professional bodies and other useful organisations consult www.buildingconservation.com/directory.html

National heritage agencies

English Heritage
☎ 0870 333 1181
✉ customers@english-heritage.org.uk
www.english-heritage.org.uk*

Cadw: Welsh Historic Monuments
☎ 01443 336000
✉ cadw@wales.gsi.gov.uk
www.cadw.wales.gov.uk

Historic Scotland
☎ 0131 668 8600
✉ Hs.grants@scotland.gsi.gov.uk
www.historic-scotland.gov.uk

Environment and Heritage Service Northern Ireland
☎ 028 9054 3064 or 028 9054 3073
✉ hbgrants@doeni.gov.uk
www.ehsni.gov.uk

National development agencies

England: Regional Development Agency (RDA)
Find your local RDA
www.englandsrdas.com

Wales: Welsh Development Agency
☎ 01443 845500
www.wda.co.uk

Scotland: Scottish Enterprise
☎ 0141 228 2000
www.scottish-enterprise.com

Northern Ireland: Invest Northern Ireland
☎ 028 9023 9090
www.investni.com

National amenity societies

Society for the Protection of Ancient Buildings (SPAB)
37 Spital Square, London E1 6DY
☎ 020 7377 1644
✉ info@spab.org.uk
www.spab.org.uk

The Georgian Group
6 Fitzroy Square, London W1T 5DX
☎ 020 7529 8920
✉ info@georgiangroup.org.uk
www.georgiangroup.org.uk

The Victorian Society
1 Priory Gardens, London W4 1TT
☎ 0870 774 3698
✉ admin@victorian-society.org.uk
www.victorian-society.org.uk

The Twentieth Century Society
70 Cowcross Street, London EC1M 6EJ
☎ 020 7250 3857
✉ coordinator@c20society.org.uk
www.c20society.org.uk

The Ancient Monuments Society
St Ann's Vestry Hall,
2 Church Entry, London EC4V 5HB
☎ 020 7236 3934
✉ office@ancientmonumentssociety.org.uk
www.ancientmonumentssociety.org.uk

*see website for addresses of regional offices

Other organisations

Architectural Heritage Fund
9th Floor, Alhambra House
27-31 Charing Cross Road, London WC2H OAU
☎ 020 7925 0199
🖷 020 7930 0295
✉ ahf@ahfund.org.uk
www.ahfund.org.uk

Association of Preservation Trusts (APT)
9th Floor, Alhambra House
27-31 Charing Cross Road, London WC2H OAU
☎ 020 7930 1629
🖷 020 7930 0295
✉ apt@ahfund.org.uk
www.heritage.co.uk/apt/

The Civic Trust
Essex Hall, 1–6 Essex Street, London WC2R 3HU
☎ 020 7539 7900
🖷 020 7539 7901
✉ info@civictrust.org.uk
www.civictrust.org.uk

The Civic Trust for Wales
3rd floor, Empire House
Mount Stuart Square, Cardiff CF10 5FN
☎ 02920 484606
🖷 02920 464239
✉ admin@civictrustwales.org
www.civictrustwales.org

Council for British Archaeology
St Mary's House, 66 Bootham, York YO30 7B2
☎ 01904 671 417
🖷 01904 671384
✉ info@britarch.ac.uk
www.britarch.ac.uk

The British Urban Regeneration Association (BURA)
63–66 Hatton Garden, London EC1N 8LE
☎ 0800 018 1260
🖷 020 7404 9614
✉ info@bura.org.uk
www.bura.org.uk

Development Trusts Association
1st Floor, 3 Bondway, London SW8 15J
☎ 0845 458 8336
🖷 0845 458 8337
✉ info@dta.org.uk
www.dta.org.uk

Heritage Lottery Fund
(including details of regional offices)
7 Holbein Place, London SW1W 8NR
☎ 020 7591 6000
🖷 020 7591 6271
✉ enquire@hlf.org.uk
www.hlf.org.uk

Royal Institute of British Architects (RIBA)
66 Portland Place, London W1B 1AD
☎ 020 7580 5533
🖷 020 7255 1541
✉ info@inst.riba.org
www.riba.org / www.aabc-register.co.uk

SAVE Britain's Heritage
70 Cowcross Street, London EC1M 6EJ
☎ 020 7253 3500
🖷 020 7253 3400
✉ save@btinternet.com
www.savebritainsheritage.org

Scottish Civic Trust
The Tobacco Merchants House
42 Miller Street, Glasgow G1 1DT
☎ 0141 221 1466
🖷 0141 248 6952
✉ sct@scottishcivictrust.org.uk
www.scottishcivictrust.org.uk

Ulster Architectural Heritage Society (UAHS)
66 Donegall Pass, Belfast BT7 1BU
Northern Ireland
☎ 028 9055 0213
🖷 028 9055 0214
✉ info@uahs.co.uk
www.uahs.co.uk

ACKNOWLEDGEMENTS

This Handbook was produced with invaluable contributions and help from individuals with experience in community-led regeneration of historic buildings. In particular, the editor would like to thank Lesley Bown, Dr Christopher Charlton, Kate Clark, Michael Coupe, Richard Dollamore, Geoff Merry and Hilary Weir. Special thanks to Julia Cleverdon and Sir Tom Shebbeare for their ongoing support.

King Sturge

King Sturge LLP is one of the largest international property consultancies in Europe, with a comprehensive network of over 100 wholly owned and associated offices throughout the world. Over 2,800 staff throughout these offices cover all property sectors and specialisms, including plant and machinery. In Europe, King Sturge operates in major UK commercial centres and principal mainland European cities.

The firm has specialist teams with expertise in heritage and regeneration, who have wide experience of acting for commercial, residential, and institutional clients, as well as working with communities in general. King Sturge has a knowledge and enthusiasm for dealing will the full range of heritage buildings: from Tudor timber-framed buildings to Georgian stone-built masterpieces, and on to more modern listed buildings such as London offices and art nouveau cinemas. King Sturge experts offer a wide range of skills including building conservation, business rates, development, planning, project management, sales and acquisitions, valuation.

Heritage buildings are immensely important in teaching people about the past and often add character and style to an otherwise nondescript built environment: with care they can be put to effective re-use to ensure their long term sustainable future.

For further information visit www.kingsturge.com or contact Bob Chapman: bob.chapman@kingsturge.com, telephone 01225 324105.

Heritage Lottery Fund

The Heritage Lottery Fund (HLF) enables communities to celebrate, look after and learn more about our diverse heritage. From museums and historic buildings to parks and nature reserves, to celebrating traditions, customs and history, the HLF has awarded over £3 billion to projects that open up our nation's heritage for everyone to enjoy.

For further information regarding HLF funded projects and grant applications visit www.hlf.org.uk or contact the Helpline on 020 7591 6042.

Sponsors

Regeneration Through Heritage is grateful for grant aid sponsorship and financial support from English Heritage, the Heritage Lottery Fund, Amersham plc, McArthurGlen Designer Outlets, Left Bank Village (Hereford), Heron Land Developments, Dr and Mrs Albert Heijn and Dr Eileen Guggenheim.